ACT III

RICHARD ROMANUS

ACT III

A small island in the Aegean

ARMIDA
AIORA

Armida Publications,   AIORA PRESS
P.O.Box 27717,   11 Mavromichali Street,
2432 Engomi, Nicosia - Cyprus -or- Athens 10679 - Greece
info@armidapublications.com   info@aiora.gr
www.armidapublications.com   www.aiora.gr

Summary:
A successful Hollywood couple decides that if life is structured like a movie,
then why shouldn't the last act be spent indulging themselves in the hopes of realizing
any leftover dreams? So the couple sells their house, pack up all of their belongings,
and together with their large black standard poodle, Guido, and twenty-two boxes
start their last act by deciding to go merrily on their way to no place in particular
until they find paradise.

[1. Personal Memoirs - Biography & Autobiography. 2. Literary - Biography & Autobiography.
3. Entertainment & Performing Arts - Biography & Autobiography. 4. Rich & Famous -
Biography & Autobiography. 4. Composers & Musicians - Biography & Autobiography.
5. Europe / General - Travel. 6. Europe / Greece - Travel.]

ISBN-13 (paperback): 978-9963-706-06-8

Front cover images - From right to left: Anthea receiving a lifetime achievement award by the Costume Designers
Guild of America (Getty Images), As Frank Vincenzo in "Murphy's Law" with Charles Bronson (Golan-Globus
Productions), As Emir Khalid Bin Abdul Majid in "Protocol" with Goldie Hawn (Warner Brothers),
Anthea as the costume designer of "F.I.S.T." with Sylvester Stallone (United Artists).

Back cover images – From right to left: Dinner with the owner of the taverna Amphiliki with Anthea and Kurt
Russell, Stopping on a walk to take in the view from the Kastro, Relaxing at Kanapitsa (Susan B. Landau).

Second edition, September 2011

Cover design by Michele Traversa | Book design by Haris Ioannides

CONTENTS

PREFACE 9

Ready or Not 13

The Road Less Travelled 25

Roots 36

A Man and His Olive Trees 44

Friends 48

Siga Siga 59

The Evil Eye 80

And the Livin' is Easy 93

Selegoudi 112

Getting Involved 119

Ohi Day 128

Quiet Time 142

Kounistra 149

'Tis the Season 157

Wonderland 170

To the Holy Mountain 180

Skiathos V. Skopelos 197

Two Goat Herders from Hollywood 205

Holiday of Holidays 213

Once You Live on a Small Greek Island 232

ACKNOWLEDGMENTS 239

PREFACE

There are two times in your life when the world is your oyster. The first is the day you decide your formal education is over and you take responsibility for yourself. The second is when you retire. In between, opportunities present themselves which you gladly take advantage of, but which make your world increasingly smaller and you more concentrated on acquiring and protecting what you've acquired. This book is what my life was like as a result of that second oyster moment. In retirement, besides the challenge of making any leftover dream come true, I soon discovered you unwittingly take on the most important job of your life: discovering who you really are, stripped from how you are defined by society.

Oh to be a frog, my lads,
and live a life free from care.

Theocritus

READY OR NOT

It's the things you say "yes" to that change your life. The "no's" lead nowhere. Anthea and I were talking about that very thing the day we were interrupted by a phone call from the Writers Guild of America who told us we had just been nominated for Best Original Screenplay in Longform Television. Anthea had been nominated and had even won a number of awards in other categories in film, having been at different times a highly successful costume designer, a vice-president at two major film studios, a producer, and finally a screenwriter. I had been a musician, actor, screenwriter, and a producer but had never been nominated for anything except class clown in high school, which I lost. So when the Guild sent us an application to submit our Christmas comedy for award consideration, I tossed it out. Anthea picked it out of the trash and sent it in. Now, while I sat stunned, she was grinning and doing a little dance. I let her have her moment, then: "The perfect second act curtain, don't you think?"

She stopped, confused. On our twentieth anniversary, over several bottles of wine, we had agreed that if a life could be measured in three acts, after the struggle to be good children in the first, to learn and produce and be good parents in the second, the last act, the shortest, should be spent for ourselves and it should begin on a high happy note. For me, there would probably never be one higher. I also knew the lure of applause, having once been caught bowing after the applause had ended and people were standing only because they were leaving.

"If not now, when?"

She blinked at me with plaintive almond eyes as if she was seven. I let the question linger until she understood, before I nodded to the seven year old and smiled paternally, whereupon the room suddenly brightened and our black standard poodle, Guido, looked up. Anthea, on the other hand, was shrinking like a flower being sucked dry by a bee. Change unnerved her. I laughed softly to calm her, gently holding but barely touching her petite frame. She took a small gasp of air. After thirty-five years as friends, lovers and partners, she knew I would try to convince her that our long second act should end here. It made perfect sense. We had saved a few dollars. We could find a wonderful place somewhere on the planet where I could write or not write, where she might paint something besides a chair. But I didn't need to convince her. After forty years of making creative decisions and solving problems, sometimes even in her sleep, she was ready for a rest. Beneath the exhilaration a gnawing sadness: we would be giving up so much, friends, family, familiarity. Yet, for the first time, we would be utterly free, able to go merrily on our way to no place in particular. We would have no plan other than freedom. Everything would be on the table, and if we didn't like where we had landed, why we'd simply try somewhere else.

When Anthea finally spoke, it was with her tiniest voice:

"But where will we go?"

I was already on the Internet:

"How about Italy!"

One of those leftover dreams which haunted me from the moment I stood in a field above the small picturesque fishing village of Porto Ercole in Tuscany and first saw the Mediterranean. Having made some extra money that year, I also realized where

I wanted to put it: four hundred rolling acres with a fifteenth century farmhouse that was on the hill behind me. The property had been abandoned, the house needed to be completely restored and updated and the land was being used by the neighbors as a cow pasture, but it was priced to steal and it already had plans and permits for restoration and update. We could take decades to do the work, and finally we'd have an elegant and beautiful home and a wonderful piece of Italy when we retired.

I held Anthea's hand and led her through a minefield of cow pies to see it. Of course she saw nothing but the cow pies and begged me to keep looking as it was the first piece of property I had seen. I looked at a dozen others but nothing remotely compared, and when we arrived back in Hollywood I immediately phoned the real estate agent in Italy who informed me the property had been sold. Twenty-five years later, I still rued that day and never listened to Anthea regarding property again. But now I was scanning international real estate rental websites looking for a life and insisting Anthea decide where it should begin:

"What about Pisa, a farm house? France, by a river? A view of the sea in Provence with a little guest house?"

After a week of indecision, Anthea quietly offered:

"Why not try Greece?"

"Greece?"

It was curious. Even though she had been raised in Brooklyn largely by her immigrant Greek grandmother, *Yiayia* Maria, Anthea had run away from her roots ever since she had been old enough to catch the subway to Manhattan.

"I just think it's practical to go somewhere where one of us speaks the language."

I couldn't disagree. Besides, what could be better than lying on a little orange and blue Greek boat with a fishing line wound around my toe?

It was several days before we were comfortable enough to

tell another person, which gave it a new cold reality. When we told yet another, we knew there was no going back because now if we didn't move to Greece, we would appear totally without a rudder. As the circle became wider and the questions became narrower, Anthea buried her anxiety beneath a list she was now making as we quickly narrowed the search to two islands off central Greece.

While most Greek islands were largely rock, these appealed to us because they were small and green. They were part of Pelion, a mountain range on the mainland where in ancient Greece the Gods were thought to go to refresh themselves among the pines, where the mountain range went under the sea and rose again as Skiathos Island, its neighbor, Skopelos, and a series of smaller islands. Anthea preferred Skiathos because it had an airport, which was exactly why I preferred Skopelos, whose citizens turned the airport down because they were afraid the island would be overrun by tourists. But Anthea argued persuasively, endlessly:

"The International Herald Tribune and London Times, which has my Cryptic Crossword, are only available on Skiathos which has a much larger village with so many more amenities, and besides, we might need to medivac out..."

So the decision was made: our first stop on our way to no place in particular would be Skiathos Island, the westernmost island of the Northern Sporades archipelago in the middle of the northeastern Aegean, forty-four miles from the nearest port on the mainland. Measuring less than four by six miles north to south, seventy percent of which was a pine forested mountain range dotted with olive groves, the island was surrounded by seventy bays, inlets and beaches ranging from golden sand sheltered by pines to white polished stones against rugged cliffs accessible only by water. It enjoyed an excellent Mediterranean climate, had a permanent population of less than six thousand, two thousand of which were expatriates from around the world, and because in the summer it was a tourist destination, almost everyone spoke the international language, English… every new fact made my pulse quicken.

Family who were friends and friends who were family were the hardest to tell. Our son Robert's response was the most piercing. He had been living on his own for several years after college and was happy for us, genuinely, but saddened for himself and his future family, knowing we'd probably never come back with any regularity. We promised it would never be a burden to him. We would see to it. Instead, he should think of the time we'd be able to spend together, strings of days and nights far from the stress of the everyday world, time to be together and play, to reflect together and argue, to teach each other what we've learned. But he didn't buy it. Tall and dark, with arms and shoulders only recently wider and stronger than my own, the vanishing little boy was knocked back on his heels. Having begun a career in film, his future was by no means certain, and he was convinced that just when he needed us most we were going to step behind a curtain and disappear. Even the house he had grown up in was on the market, the final no-going-back step. To that end, we enlisted the help of a well-known real estate agent who pulled into our driveway in a red Ferrari looking like a movie star, tanned and smiling with big white teeth. I had bought the house twenty years ago while Anthea was in Czechoslovakia, working for United Artists as the executive overseeing Barbra Streisand's production of *Yentl*.

Having learned my lesson in Tuscany, I bought it without her seeing it. It stood among huge estate trees on the very first street in Hollywood, Camino Palmero, which was designed and built in 1916 by a then famous director of silent films. On one side was the estate built by Max Factor, the theatrical makeup tsar, on the other, the house where Ozzie and Harriet Nelson lived. They had its interior duplicated on a sound stage as the set for their very popular television show, *The*

Adventures of Ozzie and Harriet, so that their children, David
and Ricky, would feel at home when they were acting in the
series. I bought the house from the estate of Will Thornberry,
who was Ozzie and Harriet's neighbor on the show, so our
house was known as "Thorny's House", an elegant, two story,
five bedroom California Craftsman Bungalow with a half acre
of lawn, a guest house, pergola and pool, and the distinction
of being on the cover of a defunct style magazine about Los
Angeles, and I thought it would sell in a day to some new TV
guy who was making a pile of money.

Selling our house from under us was deeply destabilizing.
First, the salesman listed all the clean ups and touch ups and fix
ups that had to be done before he would even begin showing
it, ugly little things and places we'd never noticed, and for the
first time we began to look at our charming nest like a whore
with runny makeup. But we dressed and fixed and painted and
planted, and Anthea placed two lemons and a knife on a cutting board next to the sink in the sparkling spotless kitchen the
day our salesman held an open house for other brokers.

"Bake bread in the oven in the morning", one salesman confided to me as he pointed to the lemons, "It'll make the buyer
feel homey."

An endless series of showings followed, during which
Anthea worked fourteen hour days, sorting books, tapes, CD's,
DVD's, clothes, memorabilia, documents, listing them as well
as making lists of everything we might need to survive on a
small Greek island. Between chores, I tirelessly surfed the web
for more information about Skiathos…"called by the same
name at least since the ancient geographer Strabo in 34 B.C.
The first village was believed to be pre-Hellenic, colonized by
the Pelasgians from Thrace who were struck by the shade provided by the huge pines. After the Pelasgians, it was the My-
cenaeans who built a village near the port and surrounded it
with a large protective wall of marble, which survived until the

Middle Ages. It was upon that ancient site that the village of Skiathos currently stood…"

The more I learned, the more alluring the island became and I began daydreaming about strolling with Anthea down old stone streets, combing lonely beaches for ancient artifacts. Life without stress.

The night of the Writers Guild Awards, we were sitting in formal dress in the ballroom of the Beverly Hilton Hotel when actress Glenn Close read the names of the four nominees in our category. I thought we probably wouldn't win, though we would no doubt have come in a close second. Preparing to overcome my disappointment I was surprised to hear:

"There's a tie!"

My whole body swelled as I looked at Anthea and slipped my hand in my pocket searching for my just-in-case-we-won speech and braced to stand. Then I heard the name of the writer of the popular miniseries I thought would win, after which Glenn Close paused to draw out the tension, which allowed me time to bring the first line of my speech, a guaranteed laugh, into my head; and then she said another name. Not ours. Oh, well. We took the loss as a sign. The next day, our agency called to tell us our agent had a nervous collapse and would be out of the office for around six months. As Anthea jotted down the address where we could send flowers, any remaining doubt about the timing of our retirement evaporated.

Then, one day, our home was sold to a new TV producer making a pile of money and we had ninety days before we would be out on the street. There was suddenly so much to do, so many loose ends there was no time to ponder the insanity of our life. More and more our future was taking shape. I was now in regular contact over the Internet with a retired American couple on the island who had raised four children in Damascus and Athens teaching in American schools, and a real estate agent from Skiathos, Geof, an Englishman, who found us a beautiful villa above the village, with a swimming pool, to rent for six months. All were welcoming and we took comfort in knowing we were already making friends. They quoted grocery store and restaurant prices, gave us information about visas, and advised us to sell our cars in Los Angeles rather than ship them to Greece and pay import duties and then have them altered to European standards. Besides, neither car seemed appropriate for a small island of mostly dirt roads. And what if we decided not to stay?

We immediately put our two cars up for sale and were having lunch at a sidewalk café when I saw a car that looked exactly like Anthea's classic convertible go by driven by a man with a large mustache:

"Look, it's exactly like yours! I've never seen another one that color." The next time we saw it was with other stolen classics on the floor of the driver's warehouse in pieces, not enough of them to make a whole car again, but enough for Anthea to put the key in the door and turn the lock in order to identify it for the insurance company. We were saddened but relieved: one car down, one to go. Several weeks later, my little black sports car was stolen from a used car lot and for a moment Anthea became concerned our name would turn up on a roster somewhere of possible insurance scammers. But there were so many things still to be done, so much to dispose of, we were just grateful that two more items were checked off from one of Anthea's lists.

I was now spending more and more time on the Internet, "...during the Persian Wars, Skiathos was one of the few islands that refused to surrender and the island served as an outpost to monitor movements of the Persian fleet." I found someone in New Jersey who knew about electric current converters and what we would need for whatever electrical appliances we would be taking, because Greece and Europe are 220 and the U.S. 110. Why can't we all just use the same current! When I finally talked to him on the phone, he spoke with a thick New Jersey accent and recommended electrical surge protectors for the current converters and I was certain I was dealing with some hustler from the Gambino Crime Family, but a week later, a box of current converters and surge protectors arrived with each item marked for what appliance. This "merrily on your way to no place" was not as easy to do as to say. And all the time Anthea kept sorting and making more lists with cross references to other lists while I kept surfing, searching, learning, "…in 42 B.C., Marc Anthony gave Skiathos to the Athenians after the Battle of Phillipi as a reward for their friendship, and the island soon became a place of exile and a hideout for Saracen pirates and thieves." Pirates and thieves began to appear in my night dreams and now I wondered if perhaps we had chosen our new neighbors and friends too hastily.

I began checking the weather on the island every day, especially those last weeks before the move: seventy-two and sunny every single day, even in late November. Although it was rainy in California, we were both feeling like the tarot card, The Fool, who has all his belongings tied into a kerchief on a stick and with his dog at his feet is staring up at the sky, smiling, while stepping off a cliff. But we both concealed it by telling each other we could hardly wait. Our arrival date would be December 28th, so we wisely shipped our heavy winter clothes on ahead along with twenty-two boxes of pots, pans, pillows and other necessities like our espresso machine.

On December 15th, the temperature on Skiathos dropped a degree. Not noteworthy. The next day another degree. Noteworthy but barely. The next day five degrees, and the next another five, and the next, and now we began to question the wisdom of sending our heavy winter clothes on an eight week journey when we might be needing them a week from Sunday. The departure day was racing toward us with increasing speed and I was frantically running around while Anthea stayed home on the phone, constantly making even more lists in an attempt to reduce the number of lists. It seemed to calm her. We now began to rely on very close friends, the ones we could call on a stormy night to get out of a warm bed and go to the Ready Teller machine at four in the morning for cash towards my bail for traffic warrants, friends to help us tag, classify, and arrange items for what seemed like the largest Christmas garage sale in history, boxes of theatrical memories, suits that would never again fit, out of style dresses and coats, thirty years of shopping and saving and being reminded not to throw anything away because someone in our past, a grandmother or an aunt, probably a child of the depression, taught us: "There's nothing a house doesn't need except illness."

In the middle of the great sale, I received a call from the production office of "The Sopranos" on which I had a recurring role. They needed me for one short scene, which would be shot in New York one day before our moving day. I was reluctant to leave Anthea in such chaos, but they agreed to fly me in on the red eye, shoot the scene in the morning, then put me back on a plane which would land in Los Angeles that same afternoon. I only had a few lines, which I planned to learn on the flight, but I was so exhausted and anxious I couldn't concentrate. Again in my hotel room, after setting my bag down, I took out my script and lay on the bed and promptly fell asleep for an hour which was when I had to meet my driver in the lobby. I quickly learned the few lines on the drive to the studio. In the scene I would be looking at a news clip on a television showing a street brawl between two groups of Italians. Only one line was giving me trouble:

"This could be scored by Albinoni's adagio."

The company was ready to shoot when I arrived. After a quick block and camera rehearsal, the director called "action", whereupon I said the few pleasantries that were written, then

noticed the television, screwed up my face with the proper concern, then moaned:

"This could be scored by Abalone's adagio!"

Someone on the crew laughed. The director stepped from
behind his monitor:

"Cut. I believe it's Albinoni's adagio. Let's go again right
away."

"This could be scored by Albinoni's alleg–agio!"

"Let's go again right away."

"Al Baloney's adagio!"

"Again right away!"

I just couldn't keep poor Albinoni or his adagio in my brain,
so the assistant director wrote it in large letters on a piece of
cardboard and placed it over the screen of the television which,
after they adjusted the camera, was out of view but perfect for
my eye line. It took five more takes before the words tumbled
out correctly and I was applauded by the crew and whisked
back to the airport.

Running through the terminal with only a few minutes to
make my plane, desperately looking for the nearest men's room,
I finally reached one only to discover it was temporarily closed.
An attendant mopping the floor kicked the sign aside when he
saw me, invited me in, then followed me to the urinal where,
while I peed, he offered several suggestions for the Sopranos
that I should pass on to the producers.

In the meantime, on the Internet the temperature on Skiathos continued to drop until the day we were moving, and on
the screen was a big black cloud over the island with many
white dots and the word blizzard. And then to see all our precious things wrapped, boxed, crated, and carried off in a truck,
and to walk around the damp empty shell with Guido, checking that we had accounted for every last piece of furniture,
every tool, plant, even the fish in the fishpond - the new owners

were cementing it over - already missing the sweet house, the dear family and friends, the privileged life, saddened by leaving, and filled with anxiety about bringing Anthea and Guido into a blizzard on an island whose ancestors were pirates and thieves and that we had never seen and knew so little about, yet feeling so completely energized, like being shot out of a cannon, liberated, like anything goes, c'mon life, let's get it on! But I didn't dare linger. Anthea, listless for the first time in forty years, was waiting outside in a rental car in the rain with four pieces of luggage and Guido's carrying case.

THE ROAD LESS TRAVELLED

To him who is in fear everything rustles.

Sophocles

It is generally agreed that the anticipation of any given event is usually greater than the realization. This was the thought racing through my mind as I held Guido close on his leash on the cold deck of an enormous ferry approaching Skiathos. Peering around the corner of the bulkhead into an icy wind to get a first glimpse of our new island paradise, I was utterly disenchanted. Not as many pines as I had hoped, a few scattered villas, roofs with tiles missing, fallen trees, broken railings, torn awnings, small rundown hotels and homes littering the shoreline. It certainly wasn't the ideal I saw on the Internet. Everything was so frighteningly third world I wouldn't have been surprised to learn pirates were still actually living there. For a moment, I clung to the hope that I wasn't being fair to this small battered island, that I was seeing the worst of it and I was just tired and sour from the journey. But as the big boat plowed along the coast past more of the same, I was already planning the renegotiation of the lease on the villa. I knelt on the deck and put my arm around Guido and scratched his chin. It never occurred to me that our merry life to nowhere in particular could possibly lead into a never-ending series of hells.

It was Guido's first time flying and he had spent fourteen hours in his carrying case until we convinced the airline to release him so we could walk him in Milan, then another eight hours until we let him out in Athens. For the first few days he wouldn't bark. Anthea noticed it first. He had lost his bark. It would finally return in a few days when we were settled, but for now he was leaning against me, freezing on the deck of the ferry, staring at Skiathos. And I, with an almost overwhelming sadness it was all my fault that I had uprooted Anthea and Guido and brought them here, was certain that Anthea had really only agreed to this madness because of me.

Suddenly, it was hailing hard and Guido and I dashed back to the cabin. Struggling to open the door against the wind, I caught a glimpse of Anthea sitting calmly, half smiling, charmed by a book of short stories written by one of Greece's most celebrated prose writers, Alexandros Papadiamantis, a native of Skiathos who wrote over a hundred short stories about the island in the early twentieth century. After squeezing through the door, I sat close to her, casually hooking her arm and smiled reassuringly as Guido curled anxiously into a ball on my feet and gave me a look.

After a few moments, the ferry passed a small island called the Bourtzi, which was filled with tall pine trees that surrounded a castle and which introduced the main port. In 1204, the Crusaders established their rule over Skiathos and left it to be governed by the Venetians, who built the castle in 1207 as a residence for governors and a citadel for the townspeople, and who retained control of the island with only a few minor interruptions until 1538, when the Turkish pirate, Khayr-ad-din-Barbarossa, Redbeard, captured it after a six-day siege.

"That must be the Bourtzi!", I tried to sound cheerful as we gathered our things.

The moment of truth was coming quickly. At the port in Skiathos, we waited inside our rented car while the huge ferry unloaded and the last tractor-trailer had left when, after a long eerie silence, we agreed the woman who was supposed to meet us and bring us the keys to the villa wasn't there. It was five days after Christmas and the ugly little village was under a blanket of dirty snow and broken tent scaffolding. We slowly drove down the deserted main street, silently looking up and down other equally deserted streets, wipers slapping against the wind and hail. Windows were shuttered or boarded and, except for a small grocery in an alleyway, there was no sign of life. We finally stopped in front of a plywood sealed store with a broken awning to form plan B but without a clue where to start. Trying to keep calm, I was startled by the appearance of two young girls, barely twenty, walking arm in arm around the corner. They smiled when they saw us and I rolled down the window and held up my hand. Using my best Greek accent, I spoke the name of the woman who was supposed to meet us.

"Excusa me. Elaine-a Bromwell? A-Geof???"

"Geof's our father!" the girls laughed in perfect English, "And where is Elaine? Wasn't she supposed to meet you? The island's a mess. We've just had the worst snow storm in fifty years!"

Everything suddenly brightened. An older couple stepped out of a doorway and waved at the girls, who waved back. As Anthea introduced Guido, a man on a motorbike passed by. Skiathos now seemed bustling and friendly and even held a certain charm as quaint Greek architecture came into focus through the dirty snow. I lay my head back on its rest, relieved that we wouldn't have to sleep in the car.

One of the more charming accidents of a small town is that everybody knows everybody. On a small Greek island everybody is also related to everybody. There are a dozen Yiorgos Mitselos but only one Elaine and one Geof, and in a moment we were ushered into the only taverna by the sea which was open in the winter, where one of the owners, a Greek American woman, Dimitra, welcomed us with a Boston accent and open arms, including Guido, then served us the best espresso we'd had in three days and wouldn't let us pay.

Within fifteen minutes, there was one long table with a dozen Skiathans and expatriates speaking English with different accents, including Geof and Elaine, whose car broke down on the road, which was why she was late and she didn't have a cell phone, but now she was going to get one:

"It's time."

With a Cheshire smile she assumed all was forgiven, and it was. Some were drinking beer and eating peanuts and some sipping ouzo and eating mezethes. It was eleven o'clock in the morning and the sun was suddenly shining and the view out to sea was astonishing, and for the first time since I left our empty house in Hollywood, a little piece of me stopped shaking. I was again feeling energized, loose, liberated, light. This was it, my new life for the next six months and I had just begun living it. And so far it was glorious.

The winding white-knuckle drive in the snow up to the top of a peninsula to our new home, the Villa Thalia, revealed a spectacular view of the village and the sea. Stopping several minutes for a large goatherd to pass, we held hands like honeymooners and watched the dogs rein in the strays and the goat herder, an old weathered man, carrying a staff and a portable radio, as he shouted at this one and that one. It had an unreality to it, like being on a movie set with the goat herder perfectly cast and where action had been called but there was no camera. We sat silently, looking out at the glistening sea, and watched the goat herder shake his staff and whistle and shout some more until they all disappeared into the overgrowth, charmed that this was our new neighborhood. Crossing through the gate of the villa revealed a view to the sea and neighboring islands as dramatic and beautiful as I'd ever seen. Inside the handsome two-story villa, the living room was quite large with marble floors, a very high ceiling and a charming fireplace, just like the pictures on the Internet. By now

I was ready to renegotiate a longer lease and chuckled to myself at our good fortune, a steal for six months at four hundred dollars a month, including water and electricity.

The villa was freezing and we soon discovered there was no central heat and no wood for a fire and only one small kerosene heater. Turning on the oven and stove burners hardly seemed to even warm the kitchenette, let alone the icy marble floors, foot thick walls, and very high ceilings. The sun was going down by the time I could scour the yard for wood and return with an armful too wet to burn, and we soon ran out of paper trying. With all the lights turned on to help heat the room and an ineffective kerosene heater at our feet, we froze that first endless night, cuddled under a thin blanket in our clothes, three of us in the same strange bed, too tired from the long journey to stay awake but too cold to sleep. I rose in the morning in a rage.

"We're outa here! Call Geof!"

Anthea, whose family came from the hills near Sparta, where women were bred to be as strong as the men, looked over at me with a yawn:

"Now, don't be a baby. Go buy some electric heaters."

Grateful for a reason to be in the car with the heater blasting, I slowly made my way down the mountain to the village. It was a blustery day and the water was grey and foamy and the village, which covered two hills, looked like a postcard of snow-draped white houses with red tiled roofs to the sea. It was calming.

In the village, I bought two large electric heaters and arranged for a load of firewood which couldn't be delivered for three days, because there was no dry wood on the island. By bedtime, with the new heaters, oven, stove burners, and lights, everything running on high, we were finally able to take off our coats. The useless kerosene heater ended up warming one side of the toilet. By morning, we were able to take off our sweaters, which was also when we realized we had spent all our drachmas on heaters and were down to our last thousand, where three hundred and eighty equaled a dollar. I quickly drove down to the bank where I discovered it would be closed for six days, as the country was now changing from the currency they had been using since the first millennium B.C., the drachma, to the euro. All we had was American dollars and Travellers Checks, and I soon realized that nobody would take either, since nobody knew what the exchange rate would be when the banks finally opened, and in a cash society no one takes credit cards, let alone American Express or personal checks.

I stood staring at a pay phone outside the bank. We had no real friends here and no money, no way to get money and no history on the island, and we needed many things, not just food, gas, and firewood. We needed heavy winter jackets, boots and wool socks, kerosene for that miserable little heater, a Greek phone, a stamp from the police to insure we had entered the country legally as no one bothered to stamp our passports when we entered Greece or even noticed Guido. We were trapped.

When I was twenty-one, I left law school and went to New York City to be a folk singer. The city was cold and confusing and having quickly spent most of the few hundred dollars I had saved on a roach infested hotel just below Times Square, my guitar and I spent a number of weeks on the subways until I found a job as a clerk in a leather factory on the lower East Side and could finally settle myself. But I was young and could exist on candy bars and cigarettes. I was also fearless and had more faith in my wits. I could also speak the language.

Anthea's father was a major supplier of butter, eggs, and gourmet foods to the better hotels and restaurants in New York City and she grew up on caviar and cashmere sweaters. She had her own credit card when she was eleven and was allowed to go alone by taxi to shop for her clothes at Martin's Department Store.

Her first costume job was to assist the designer for the original production of the longest running musical in theatre history *The Fantastiks*. Her first Hollywood movie as costume designer was Roman Polanski's *Rosemary Baby*. She led a charmed life and had never gone without. But she was a Spartan, and she was smarter than me. Without knowing it at first, I later realized I preferred it that way. Together we made a perfect person. She would be the brains. I would be tall enough to get a plate from the top shelf.

By the time I returned to my car, I had talked myself back to calm. Anthea would know what to do. But for the moment I wasn't certain I had enough fuel to make it back up the mountain, so I decided to give begging a shot and stopped at the gas station. After stepping out in the snow in a cotton sweater and loafers, I turned my pockets inside out to the attendant, a tall, gentle, soft spoken man in his early thirties with eyes that twinkled under the hood of a down jacket. He understood rather quickly that I had no money:

"No problem" he smiled amused as he picked up the pump handle. "You pay tomorrow."

Then, upon arriving back at the villa with a tank full of gas and a can of kerosene, I saw Anthea in the doorway, explaining in the Greek of a six-year-old to a taxi driver, who had arrived with a trunk load of his personal firewood, that we were very sorry but we couldn't pay him the eleven thousand drachmas he was promised:

"No problem" he returned in accented English, then handed me his card as he carried an armload through the snow and stacked it by the steps. "Call me if you need anything. Thanassis, like Onasis. You know, Onasis?"

After six days, we would also owe Geof fifty thousand drachmas, Dimitra the tab for half a dozen meals at her taverna as well as fifty thousand, which she thrust upon us for walking around. We even owed the police ten thousand for stamping our papers and weren't they surprised when I arrived the morning the bank opened to pay up.

"You didn't have to come today!"

Climbing down the flight of steps from the police station, I couldn't help but laugh in disbelief. Where on earth had we landed where without hesitation, without questioning, without exception, people opened their hearts and wallets to complete strangers?

In Greek mythology, Zeus, in human form, and his son Hermes, without his wings, presented themselves at every door in the village of Phrygia, seeking rest and shelter from the cold night, but all the people were inhospitable and turned them away until they came upon the humble dwelling of Philemon and Bacchus, a penniless old couple, who welcomed them and cheerfully served them what little they had. As Philemon was pouring the last of his wine, he was astonished to see the pitcher immediately refilled. Recognizing their heavenly guests, they fell on their knees begging forgiveness for their meager offerings. The Gods praised them for their virtue, then took them to the highest hill where they saw the whole unwelcoming village of Phrygia sink under a lake. Only their house was left standing, which the Gods then turned into a temple with columns and a gilded roof.

I would soon realize that every child on the island grew up knowing that myth. It was, after all, part of their history, a teaching tool from the ancients, who believed that for their own well-being the love of strangers was equal in importance to the love of wisdom. The sweet surprise for me was how much their ancient ancestors still lived in these people. After only a handful of days in this new place with its strange language and alien alphabet, I felt safe, secure, familiar, as if I'd come home after a long absence and, although no one recognized me, it still held the same innocence and generosity I had been longing for.

As I climbed into my rented car, I was reminded of a thought I had read somewhere that there was an inverse proportion between civilization and the distance from the Mediterranean. As I drove away, I was more and more convinced of the wisdom in it.

That night, having paid our creditors, Anthea and I finally felt organized enough to take a walk through the village, down narrow stone streets, up a dozen old stone steps to the square of the Cathedral of the Three Hierarchs lit with Christmas lights, where children were playing tag and kicking soccer balls in the snow. It was a magical walk, silent, arm in arm, the air cold, crisp and clean, snow crunching beneath our feet, passing a small butcher shop, a bakery where a man was sitting behind the counter playing a *bouzouki*, feeling as though our dream had somehow come true. Stopping at a small picturesque taverna in a centuries' old stone house with wonderfully simple Greek food, we ordered fresh fish on the grill, a green salad, fries, and thin red local wine, all of it just as I had imagined. In the corner, several Greeks in layered wool and hats, fisherman drinking ouzo, and a family of three, one a small boy with very thick glasses who reminded me of me when I was his age, probably four, was eating a French fry, laughing quietly with his father.

Crossing back under the simple strings of Christmas lights in the now empty square of the Three Hierarchs, Anthea seemed quietly joyful as she absently began humming a song she had heard on the radio, her voice deep, her pitch not always perfect, but heartfelt.

Once on location in Toronto, sitting at a hotel bar with a few of the crew at the end of a long shooting day, someone asked me to describe my wife.

"Anthea" I answered as if I had been waiting to be asked for twenty years. "Well, she's tougher than most guys, but she's more feminine and beautiful than most women. She's smarter than most people, funnier than most comics, she cooks better than most gourmet chefs, is celebrated for her taste, and she's crazy about me." That's my girl.

We slowly moved down the wide stone stairs and along the port where fishing boats bobbed in the water under a sky so clear and filled with stars you could clearly see the Milky Way. Then the big bell from the church interrupted Anthea and continued until we counted to ten, whereupon she resumed humming as we continued down the quay to the car. That was the night I fell in love with Skiathos.

The next day, we left on the ferry for Athens to drop off our rental and pick up our new car. I bought the first car I looked at in Athens while en route to Skiathos, but we had to wait a week to take delivery while the dealer processed the papers. I thought it looked "islandy", a used red and white canvas topped four-wheel drive Suzuki. Later in the summer, I would discover that every other rental car in Skiathos was an "islandy" red and white canvas topped Suzuki.

It was a relief to get away from Skiathos for a few days. It provided a rare chance for me to reflect on the events of the past few weeks. In spite of the changes and challenges, some of which had sent me spinning, Anthea seemed to be effortlessly shifting into an anxiety-free gear, as if knowing in advance it would all be easily settled.

Although originally planning to spend only two days in Athens, we ended up having to spend a week. The city was paralyzed in a blanket of white and looked quite beautiful. Everyone seemed to take time to play, old people throwing snowballs, children of all ages making huge snowmen. Anthea, Guido and I took long walks, guidebook in hand. It was astounding to see historical sites almost on top of each other, ancient Greek, Roman, Byzantine, and Turk, and Anthea and I, playful for the first time in months, threw snowballs at each other everywhere, in the Plaka where Socrates once walked with his students, in front of the final home of Lord Byron, even by the deserted Parthenon, always with some for Guido to catch with his mouth.

Finally, the ferries were running again and we sailed back to Skiathos. Arriving into the port, I was struck by how charming the village now seemed and how much it felt like I was coming home, though when we arrived at the villa half the electric outlets wouldn't work and we froze again that night. We did, however, take that wonderful walk through the village to the old taverna where the owner, Pandelis, remembered and warmly welcomed us, and where we had another simple home cooked meal, and where a large table of Skiathans had finished eating and were singing and drinking and bought us a pitcher of wine.

The past two weeks seemed like months since we last glimpsed Hollywood, but we now had a bank account, a car in the driveway, Guido was beginning to find his bark, and we were relaxed and reading Homer in front of a warm fire, heaters blasting away, piling up a monstrous electric bill for our unsuspecting landlord. Our espresso machine was on the counter with its attendant converter and protector having finally arrived, our computer was up and running, and we were looking forward to another night's walk to that taverna, where we'd have some white bean soup and a fish delivered minutes before in a blue plastic produce bag by a fisherman layered in wool, selling the day's catch, and where we'd sing along with the others and think if only our friends were here.

ROOTS

Everything comes by way of strife and necessity.

Heraclitus

The day after returning from Athens, I called Geof and asked him to show me some of the properties for sale on the island.

"Why don't you wait until you've settled in some more?"

"I don't want to wait, I want to see some now", the ugly American tried not to sound impatient.

"Meet me at twelve at the acropolis."

It was impossible not to trust Geof completely. A bit over-weight, in his fifties, with curly grey-brown hair which was always disheveled, he and his gentle freckle-faced Dutch wife, Lida, were becoming increasingly important to us. Besides responding to our calling twelve times a day for advice, they also included us in any ex patriot gatherings, as well as taking us sailing in their catamaran to neighboring islands on sun glorious days. As a young man, Geof was working as a clerk in an office in England when an aunt died and left him a small inheritance, whereupon he became a hippie and decided to see the world. Landing first in Skiathos, he never left. After marrying Lida, who he met on holiday from Amsterdam, and raising two daughters, he now had a real estate business and a Skiathos information website, which is how I found him.

I had been tracking available Skiathos properties on the Internet for months and was excited about finally seeing them. Now five minutes late, I was already agitated when I rushed out of the bank towards my jeep and, to my horror, realized it was being blocked by a new sedan that had parked perpendicular to it and without a soul in sight. I waited. One minute. Two. I was openly cursing when the bank door finally opened and a well dressed man with a briefcase, obviously not from Skiathos, ambled out and strolled towards me. The ugly American couldn't contain himself.

"Hey! Hey, is this your car! Is this your car!"

The man looked at me quizzically, then quickly sized up the situation and spoke softly in clear educated English with a slight Greek accent.

"No. But perhaps I can be of assistance."

Climbing into the car, he started the motor, backed it up six feet to free my jeep, then climbed out of the car and without looking back proceeded on his way. The ugly American couldn't let him go.

"Hey! Hey! Do you know whose car this is!?"

The man turned his head slightly, and with a small shrug, a tired smile, and a flick of his wrists he taught me an enormous lesson.

"No. It's Greece, eh?"

In Hollywood, on the afternoon when we were leaving our old life behind, Anthea, Guido and I were sitting silently in our rental car on our way to the airport, stalled in bumper-to-bumper traffic. In the lane next to us sat a shiny black Humvee, a personal car almost as big as a city bus. A man dressed in black with sculpted steel grey hair behind the wheel looked distressed as he barked into his cell phone, and I wondered if he ever thought about how quickly the clock was ticking. And then the traffic inched ahead again and I followed, wondering how I could have ever endured so much time so ill spent, counting the hours when we would be on our little island with a small simple life. Now, having left a world where stress was almost constant, I was manufacturing it in order to maintain my comfort level. The irony didn't escape me. I also felt the embarrassment of a blundering idiot as I watched my well dressed Good Samaritan continue his stroll along the quay. I was living in a country whose ancestors I had studied and admired but whose modern hosts I hadn't investigated or even tried to understand. I vowed to change that.

Following Geof in his old dented white truck, I looked at the few houses and several building sites. Knowing that I was beyond being interested in her opinion, Anthea came along for the ride and remained in the car, puzzling over her London Times Cryptic Crossword. Although on the Internet each property once seemed genuinely promising, they were sadly disappointing, not worth calling Anthea out of the car to see. Since there are very few properties for sale on a small island, I became suddenly anxious. "No stress", I said to myself, "no stress."

While another voice said "But what if you wanted to stay here?"

I had decided to call it a day when Geof suggested, if the road was passable, he'd show us a parcel he hadn't shown anybody because he had been hoping to buy it himself. Due to the storms, there were several pine trees that had fallen across the road, but Geof explained that because it was a fire road, the town usually cleared it rather quickly. It sounded too difficult to be worth the trouble, but Geof said it wasn't far and urged me to at least take a look. I was already wary when we turned onto a muddy rut-filled road and Geof told me to switch into four-wheel drive, something entirely new to me. As we splashed and sloshed around the felled trees which had been cut and dragged to the side, allowing just enough room to pass, I was sure I would never want to live at the end of it all, and that Anthea would be even less inclined. But there are those rare exceptions to the anticipation/realization rule, because after a short ride, Geof pulled to the side of a breathtaking clearing surrounded by a protected forest and populated with hundreds of olive, fig, pear, and chestnut trees. The property began on the crest of a high ridge overlooking a valley dotted with farms and olive groves, which were dusted with snow to a several mile slice of the Aegean, beyond which Euboea, the second largest island in Greece, rose out of the sea with blue and purple snow-capped mountains that seemed painted and appeared to roll on forever. I was dazzled. Tuscany, which I had idealized over the years, suddenly paled. After taking a few steps on the land, I decided it was too beautiful and too well priced at seventeen million drachmas, forty-thousand American dollars, not to buy, and when Geof said in the spring the entire countryside would be covered with red poppies, I hurried back to the car and invited Anthea to step out and look.

It was the first time we ever agreed on property.

Within two days - a little bargaining was to be expected - we two rolling stones had a deal to buy two and a quarter acres of Greece for fifteen million drachmas. We knew it would sound crazy, we hadn't been in Greece two weeks. But I couldn't walk away from it. I wanted that land, craved it. After having owned property for thirty years, being landless for a few weeks made me deeply uneasy and I longed to feel grounded again, to have a piece of earth of my own where Guido and I could walk, let alone an olive grove that I could tend to, and old stone walls where I could just sit and watch the boats go by. But buying land on Skiathos was like entering into a marriage. There were no guarantees, no escrow insurance. Even though Geof insisted we engage an attorney to research the provenance, and a notary public to attest to the fact that what we bought was what we bought, no one would accept responsibility if, and it happened from time to time, we later discovered the title was not clear because some relative also claimed ownership, or it was not two and a quarter acres, but a quarter acre. It was a handshake society with no written records of boundaries or ownership. Neighbors agreed this parcel began at that stone, followed that ridge, ended at that tree, and even though that's your fence, it runs several meters on his land and those are his olive trees. And if anyone should contest the title or boundaries, redress in court takes a decade or more and, until that time, the property in dispute cannot be claimed by anyone.

But we closed our eyes, trusted in the goodness of men, and continued. The contract itself was an interesting insight into the psyche of a people that for many centuries kept two sets of books, one for whoever was the occupying power, one for themselves. Only now the occupying power was the Greek government.

Entering Greece with an American passport only allowed us to stay three months, so a priority now was to get a visa, which would extend our stay to at least a year. In order to apply, we needed copies of our passports, proof of health insurance, which would cover hospitalization and prescriptions in Greece, proof of an income of five hundred euros a month, and finally a health certificate from a state hospital, verifying we had no contagious disease. Nothing seemed unreasonable. A copy of our passports was easy. Proof of health insurance was also simple, since they only required letters from our guilds affirming we were insured in Greece. Proof of income of five hundred euros was also not a problem. To satisfy the health certificate requirement we were advised to go to the Skiathos Health Center, a modest one story building a stone's throw from the cemetery, for an examination by the chief physician, a white haired man working well past retirement age.

Sitting in his dark, cluttered, smoke-filled office, the doctor sat silently, a cigarette dangling from his mouth as he stared over bifocals at Anthea, while she told him with her limited Greek vocabulary that we needed to be examined for any contagious diseases so that we could get a visa, whereupon he nodded, looked at us with narrowing eyes, then asked us in perfect English if we had any contagious diseases. When we shook our heads, he dropped his long ash on the floor and stamped our health certificates.

Stamps, I soon discovered, were an important part of Greek life. Every office had a clerk with a mountain of rubber stamps from which he chose at least five or six for each transaction, each requiring a signature, to which he would then affix several different colorful paper stamps on top of the images of the rubber stamps to any given document. The documents were all written by hand. At first, it seemed rather charming, but then we found ourselves having to go from this office to that office, over to that building, back to this office, back to that building, with certified translations from English to Greek of any letter or document which proved income or insurance, all the while accumulating more stamps, signatures and handwritten statements before we were able to hand in our applications. Of course each stamp had a small fee attached.

Everything appeared to be happening for the first time with any given clerk. Staring at the copy of my passport an overly long time, one man who looked like Tom Hanks' double was puzzled:

"Where's your father's name? Your father's name must be on your passport, no?"

In Greece, your father's name was very important and on every document you must list your father's name. Anthea said it was because Greece was made up mostly of small villages where there were, say, fifteen Yiorgos Skouros, and you identified which Yiorgos by his father.

"In America they don't put your father's name in your passport."

I handed him my actual passport. Staring at me curiously, the clerk picked up the phone, dialed, spoke to a superior somewhere, all the while studying every page of the passport, holding it up to the light. Then, satisfied, he hung up, looked at me, shook his head, and stamped my application several times.

From the time we first landed on the island, Anthea and I quickly began amusing ourselves by spotting doppelgangers. Besides Tom Hanks at the visa office, the man who pumped our gas looked like George Clooney, Yiorgos, our dry cleaner, like the actor Seymour Cassel. We saw James Dean, taller, a fat Walter Matthau, Hillary Clinton with chartreuse hair, Robert Downey Junior at two. After over three thousand years of almost continual conquest and occupation, reconquest and occupation, Skiathans were the result of a huge and varied gene pool and had every combination of characteristics of all the Western and Middle Eastern peoples, with hair from blonde and bright red to kinky jet black, eyes of palest blue to black, skin from pink to sun-stained olive. On the other hand, what all Skiathans physically had in common was their density. Just as I had suspected, they were a solid people. Strong. Sturdy. Physical. And yet, even though they'd had what Papadiamantis called "centuries of harrowing history of suffering and blood", they seemed to be a gentle people, humorous, generous, humble even in their pride, and stunningly content. Every clerk was quite cordial, although one day in the post office I heard one old woman complaining that she had sent a letter to Athens last week, a distance of a hundred and fifty miles, and it still hadn't gotten there.

"Has it been ten days?" Angeliki, the stern middle-aged postmistress with henna dyed hair didn't look up from sorting the day's delivery, "Then don't complain."

By now, it was the end of February and the days had suddenly turned sunny and warm. We were beginning to know our way around the village where more and more faces were becoming familiar. The legal transfer of the property moved along the strangulating Greek bureaucracy without a hitch, and we had a celebratory lunch at Dimitra's with Geof, who said it was the easiest money he ever made. By now we had also accumulated all the necessary materials for our visas with their requisite stamps and signatures and handed them in, and we were able to sit in the sun for hours on the terrace of Villa Thalia, rereading the ancient Greek playwrights, glancing up occasionally towards a small colorful fishing boat putt-putting by in the cerulean blue sea below. Hollywood seemed so very far away now, agents, studios, deals, all so insignificant, and in its place an exquisite state of grace not unlike what is carved on the gravestone of the celebrated writer Nikos Kazantzakis in Crete: "I fear nothing. I hope for nothing. I am free."

A MAN AND HIS OLIVE TREES

He is the sort that would cut down an olive tree.

Ancient insult

By the first of March the days were glorious, and Guido and I would walk on our land amidst the promised red poppies and the first leaves of the fig trees, past a group of old Judas trees with bright pink flower clusters. I had been reading about our olive trees which the land contract numbered at two hundred fifty, and which Geof estimated to be at least two hundred years old. I decided one day they needed to be shaped. A change of wardrobe and a stop at the hardware store and I was back with Guido and a small hand saw and several garden tools, dressed as an olive tree pruner.

Although there was evidence to suggest the cultivated olive was at least five thousand years old, nobody knew when, where, and who first cultivated it, but it is certain they were wanderers, perpetually trying to fend off starvation, not far from the Aegean Sea and the eastern end of the Mediterranean, the fountain of civilization. The Egyptians, Cretans, Phoenicians, Hellenes, Carthaginians, Arabs and Romans all had one common denominator, the olive tree. Besides wood for fire and weapons, the fruit from the tree allowed them to have a healthy diet all year, and its oil, stored in jars under their dwellings, was a preservative for the rare piece of meat, and also provided oil for lamps so that work and leisure could continue after dark. Without leisure it would have been impossible to have developed higher thought. Under the shade of the olive trees in Athens, democracy was born. And no matter how many times someone cut it down, burned it to the ground, ripped it out by its roots, the olive tree would come back and live for a thousand more years. No wonder the Ancients thought the tree was immortal. And now, I had my very own grove and it was no small comfort to know that no matter what happened in the world, I was assured of a healthy diet and plenty of firewood. Assuming somewhere the genes of my Lebanese ancestors would intuitively know how, I proceeded to shape several trees with my pruning shears and small saw, feeling the ancient connection, rejoicing in my good fortune. Guido watched for a moment, then became bored and wandered off to sniff.

It happened that the man who owned the land next to ours was sitting in front of his *kalivi*, small cabin, looking down on us. I hadn't noticed him before, but in a moment, Yiorgos, a bear with sparkling blue eyes and a permanent smile, was standing with Guido next to me. He took the pruning shears from my hand and stepped between me and the tree.

"*Avrio*" he gently pushed me away, "*Avrio*."

Which I thought probably meant I was destroying two hundred year old olive trees and I should leave them alone.

The next day, while sitting depressed under one of my humiliations, Guido barked and I heard a rustle behind me and was astonished to see Yiorgos step down from his land with a chainsaw, two gallons of gasoline and several cans of oil. After a "*Kalimera*", good morning, he fired up the chainsaw, stepped up to the tree next to me and proceeded to cut all the deadwood and all the suckers around the base of the trunk. Knowing Yiorgos was from an old Skiathan family, I had complete confidence in him, and made mental notes as he whacked all the big and little branches until the tree was the shape of a wine glass and, as the Skiathans say, until it was open enough for a bird to fly through it. Yiorgos moved from tree to tree while I followed in his wake, collecting the branches, working until late afternoon, cleaning and pruning all of my olive trees, certainly not two hundred and fifty, but more than I needed to run my little household. It was Yiorgos' way of both welcoming me into the neighborhood and saving those two hundred year old trees.

In Hollywood, I was unlucky enough to have had a next door neighbor living in the Ozzie and Harriet house, a doctor who advertised his breast enhancement services on television and who was a constant source of irritation, instituting a failed costly legal action to claim seven inches of my land, notifying the city that I was illegally renting a unit, when one of my brothers who had just graduated from music school was staying in our guest house for several weeks, calling the police when someone parked in front of our house, a restricted parking area, even if it was a delivery truck - a constant thorn and obviously a very unhappy man. So it was with such overwhelming gratitude that it was humbling when, after pruning my whole grove, Yiorgos invited me up to his *kalivi* for coffee, which he would continue to do from time to time. We would sit, sipping his dark, thick sweetened brew, he knowing no English, me knowing no Greek, just good neighbors, blessed, looking out at the sea, smiling, occasionally one or the other saying the one or two words I understood:

"*Kala?*" Good?

"*Poli kala.*" Very good.

There was still an hour of daylight after Yiorgos left, when Guido and I returned to our land awash in olive branches, so I decided, like every other landowner on Skiathos, to collect the branches and burn them. I had some fire starters and a Zippo and set some fairly good fires, but it took several before I realized that wind was a factor and you want to set the fire upwind of your pile of olive branches or risk losing hair. Another lesson learned was not to wear cashmere to a burning, especially downwind where the sparks will burn hundreds of tiny holes. The third and perhaps most important was to hire someone who knows what they're doing because, although I stayed until the last fire was out, when I arrived the next morning, I was dumbstruck to see a good portion of my other neighbor's land covered in ashes and two mature pine trees badly burned. Geof explained to me later that I had set one of the fires atop a very old grape vine which continued underground until reaching the neighbor's land and then rose up again. Thank God I didn't burn down the island but also for keeping any of the other Skiathans away that day, so I could hire someone to rake over the ashes and clean out the burn as much as possible before I phoned our neighbor, Thalia, who would soon become our Dentist. She said she didn't mind, she understood. Blessed on both sides.

In the fall, I would harvest a few of our olive trees which would give us enough olives for the year, but oil for only several months. It takes quite a few to produce a year's supply of oil and although the actor from Hollywood very quickly learned to look and feel like an olive picker, unfortunately he wasn't properly prepared for the part and so, after a week of picking, decided unless there was a famine or he was stone broke, one week a year of picking olives would be quite enough.

FRIENDS

It is not only fine feathers that make fine birds.

Aesop

It had been one of my life's misfortunes that all of my best friends died young. The first, a blue baby, only lived to fourteen, the second was killed in a boating accident at twenty-three, the third, the youngest head of production in the history of Warner Brothers, dropped dead on a movie set at forty-four, and the last, the youngest reporter ever on the payroll of the San Francisco Examiner, who succumbed after a heroic bout with cancer at sixty-two. When I mentioned it to Anthea she looked away and said: "The good news is they're living longer."

Each had been remarkable in his way and they had lately been in my thoughts. Their appetite for life was inspiring, yet, like Schubert's 8th Symphony, it was left unresolved, having built to a moment which would never come, a constant reminder that life was not guaranteed.

By now, I had been without a best friend for several years and, missing that comradeship more and more, I wondered if perhaps I might ever find it on Skiathos. I soon learned that when you're merrily on your way to no place in particular, making new friends is easy. Everyone wants to be loved, and when you have no other agenda it's easy to penetrate even the hardest heart. As a child I intuitively knew this when I would walk up to anyone, introduce myself, and make a friend. Most men can't believe you don't have an agenda at first. It's antithetical to them. Women are generally much more receptive, captured by the moment, although men, even if they are initially wary, like nothing more than to make a new friend, so with the smallest effort you may soon find you have too many and you begin to prune and become slightly more discriminating. At first the baker, the grocer, the bank teller all became like friends, not close enough to have to dinner, but close enough that I recognized them by name, and they seemed happy to see me and I felt a kind of friendship.

In a community of expatriates, it was even easier to make friends. The fact that we were other aliens immediately established a bond, and the other couples were always interested in meeting new couples and making new friends, adventurers all. And what a community to pick from. Besides Geof and Lida, and the teachers, Bruce and Marcia, who were the only other American couple, and Elaine who was from South Africa, there were the Romyns, an elderly English couple who left the publishing world in London to establish the most important ballet company in England, only to have their prima ballerina take over the company and move them out; the Sherwins, compulsively neurotically painting and repainting their house who, having several rental properties back in England for income, were also merrily on their way to no place in particular and within the year would sell their continually repainted house and move to France, and the list goes on and on, including expatriates from everywhere, each with their own story. Harder was making friends among the Greek community, especially on a small island where family was everything, and close friends were from childhood.

I made my first real Greek friend on the road around Koukounaries Beach, which lies on the southwestern corner of Skiathos and has been described as the most unspoiled natural beach in the Mediterranean. Bordered by large stone pine trees which yield the delicate edible nuts hidden deep inside their cones, or koukounaria, known to the rest of the world as pignoli or pine nuts, the beach itself is fine rose-colored sand, with clear clean water that gradually deepens, while in the distance the purple mountains of Euboea climb to the sky.

In the middle of the pines is Strofilia Pond, a fresh water natural habitat for migrating birds and a favorite fishing spot of many on the island. Beyond that is a small country road, which starts at one end of Koukounaries Beach with its small port crowded by a gaggle of small fishing boats. The road then winds around the pond, passing several tavernas and hotels and a horse farm, and stops at the other end in a dirt parking lot which, if you include the length of the beach, is a distance of approximately three miles.

It had become my habit to take a daily walk there with Guido. We would start by the small port, where two groups of ducks would swim back and forth, back and forth near a small wooden arched bridge, each group endlessly squabbling over territory with the other. In mid March, it was sunny but cooler when we started our walk past clusters of wild white irises hugging the pond and white heather, which lay in clumps on the side of the road. Guido ran on ahead and was out of sight when I reached the area where the small hotels and tavernas were gathered. I was buttoning up my jacket while walking past one of the smaller tavernas, in which several workmen were hammering and sawing when, out of the corner of my eye, sitting across the road on a fence post, smoking and petting Guido while tending a herd of goats grazing next to Strofilia pond, I saw a rugged looking older bull of a man in layered flannel with a weathered face and hands that obviously gripped and grabbed and held for a living. When I saw someone and our eyes met, it was my new custom to say "*Yiasou*", which means 'health to you' and is the usual greeting and appropriate parting in Greece. The man smiled broadly and

waved and spoke several sentences in Greek, while playfully
tousling Guido's head. I smiled and bowed and held up my
hand.

"Sorry, I don't speak Greek" I smiled again and backed away
smiling and waving.

"Who are you!" boomed from his barrel chest.

He stood and strode towards me with a grin, swaying from
side to side as if he were on the deck of a tall ship.

"Where you from? You English?"

"I live in Skiathos but I'm an American. From California."

"California!" he laughed loudly, "Where? San Diego? San
Pedro? San Francisco? I been there!"

"Ah, you were a seaman?"

"Fifteen years. My name Mihalis. Michael. I been to China,
you speak Chinese? Nee how ma?"

"No, I don't speak Chinese."

"Why you come Skiathos?"

"Well, we wanted to make a change."

"Change! Yes, everything changes! The air is always changing! The sea, it's always changing, the earth, always changing!
You know Erakleetus?"

"Erakleetus?"

"Erakleetus! He was Greek!"

"Erakleetus???" Suddenly, from my old philosophy major
days, "You mean Heraclitus?"

"Yes, Erakleetus! You know him?"

"Yes, of course! Everything's in a continual state of change,
Heraclitus, the earth, the sky–"

"How you know Erakleetus?"

"I studied him in school."

Mihalis smiled, pleased. I was suddenly curious about this
old goat herder, "How do you know Eracleetus? Did you learn
in school?"

"No, no. In school we learn to read and write. Thirteen

years old no more school. No high school in Skiathos, not like now. I work in town one year, helping. Then I go to work on the boats. I see the world. I was in Russia. You speak Russian?"

"No, I only speak English."

"What you do all day?"

"It's hard to explain. But you didn't tell me how you knew about Erakleetus."

"Erakleetus! When I go to work on the boats my father give his books. All Greeks. Thucydides, Homer, seventeen books, Herodotus, Aristophanes. Fifteen years away from Skiathos on the boats I read the books over and over, Pythagoras, Plato, and for I get homesick, Papadiamantis, to remind me of Skiathos."

I was touched, "Your father was very wise to give you those books."

Tears quickly formed in his eyes, "My father, yes." Mihalis was watching an eagle gliding on the wind over the pond, "You have a boat?"

"Not yet. One day I will."

"You put your boat next to mine. In Koukounaries. My boat is Argo. I'll take you fishing. You know what is Argo?"

"Yes."

He looked at me suspiciously: "You know? What is Argo?"

I tossed it off, "Jason."

He laughed loudly, "Aw, you know everything!"

From his first day on the boats and for the next four years, Mihalis worked shoveling coal in the boiler room of a freighter to save enough for a small house for his older sister's prika, or dowry, without which she probably wouldn't find a husband. When he was thirty and finally returned to Skiathos, it had changed so much Mihalis would hardly recognize it. There were no cars when he left, no paved road. Even the waterfront had dramatically changed. There were new streets, and now there was even a high school. Vacationers were beginning to come in the summer, and men from Skiathos were abandoning ships all over the world and coming home to try and make their living off their land, the sea, and the tourists.

There was no road to Koukounaries from the village when Mihalis went to sea, nothing more than a donkey path. But when he returned there was an unpaved road. It was summer and it was hot as he walked the distance of about six miles from the village to his dozen acres of land in Koukounaries, its olive trees and its summer garden. It also housed his pigs, sheep, goats, a horse, a donkey, a dozen chickens, a rooster, some rabbits, and an old *kalivi* which was cool even on a hot day. There were other people walking and some even driving to Koukounaries, and by the time Mihalis reached his land, he became convinced that if he quickly built another *kalivi*, he might be able to rent them both in the summer. Which he did. And then two more the summer after. Then ten more, and twenty more and every year a few more until he now had ninety-four rooms and two tavernas, which he supplied with meat and produce from his own animals and garden, where in the spring he would plant three thousand tomato plants for the summer season.

Now surrounded by his family and businesses, his herds and gardens, and even a grandchild, the classically self-educated Mihalis had finally come full circle and was harvesting a lifetime of hard work. The men hammering and sawing across the street were working for him while he was doing what he loved. He suddenly shook his stick and bellowed at a goat that was eating his way out of the gate, then he took my sleeve. "Tomorrow I kill a pig. Come to the taverna Saturday" he pointed across the street, "Eight o'clock. I cook. Fresh pork. Wine, I make it myself. Bring your wife! You have a wife?"

"Yes, I do."

"Childrens?"

"One son who lives in California."

"I have two sons! Bring some friends if you want!" Then he grinned and I shook his hand.

"Eight o'clock! Don't forget! I'll make fresh cheese from my goats!"

"I'll look forward to that" and I shook his hand again and continued on my way.

"*Yiasou!*"

"*Yiasou!*"

As I passed the horse farm with its newly plowed fields of rich brown earth, I thought of Mihalis' eyes at the mention of his father who, on the day he gave his son his precious books, would also be grateful that the boy would now be able to provide for himself, leaving more for his wife and two daughters. An itinerant violin player as his father before him, Mihalis' father was usually absent, traveling around the mainland, playing at weddings, looking for work every day of every year, yet barely earning enough for himself and his family, carrying the heartache of seeing his only son off to sea at fourteen, still a boy, with nothing more to give him, only his books to keep him company, yet still able to fill Mihalis with that rich kind of love that became painful when recalling him. And as I continued on my walk, there was a moment when I felt a sadness for my own father, though different, for although he was the most important influence in my life, an overwhelming presence, my sadness was for what might have been had I a father like Mihalis', whereas my own father had become simply a character in my past I'd rather forget.

A big orange sun was low in the sky, reflecting in the sea as I left the road and approached the beach. Guido came into view shaking me out of my reverie. He was chasing a horse with a young blonde girl who was skillfully riding bareback, trotting along the orange foam, a movie shot. I sat on a bench to watch the day end. I was excited. How much fun it would be eating

Mihalis' fresh pork and cheese and drinking his home made wine. I knew we would become good friends.

The sun had all but set and the colors were darkening as the horse and rider disappeared near Strofilia Pond, and Guido came trotting back towards me, tired, thirsty, and happy. I made a mental note to look for the Argo, which would be docked in the small port, then continued towards my car, thinking that some days the walk around Koukounaries was just a mile too short.

Anthea and I were so taken by the generosity of the people and the beauty of the island that, after buying the land, there was never any question we would build on it. Anthea had already been thinking about hardware even though it would be over a year before we'd need it: simple black iron doorknobs and hinges. It was at his hardware store that I first met Spiros. He showed us several books and let us bring one home where Anthea chose the simplest pattern and I returned the book with our phone number and asked him to notify me if they decided to discontinue the line because I might be ordering two exit door handles and a number of interior door and window handles in a year or so. He looked at me as though it was a sentence he had already heard several times that morning, then smiled politely as he picked up a ringing phone.

"I keep the book for you."

Slipping the book into the bottom drawer of an overstuffed desk, he moved on to tend to one of the crush waiting patiently behind me.

I next saw him walking with his wife, Matoula, on Papadiamanti Street, the main shopping street in the village which was named for the famed local writer. It was Matoula I noticed first. Even though Spiros was a tall, strikingly handsome, wholesome Greek man of forty, with a shock of black hair and a toothy grin, Matoula was his flawless female counterpart, and

I might not have noticed Spiros at all if he hadn't said *kalimera* to me.

The third time I saw him was at a restaurant. He was with Matoula and six or seven others and I remarked when they entered to Anthea, who agreed, that they were the handsomest couple on the island. After they were seated, Spiros sent over a bottle of fine wine and when it was delivered, he shyly smiled and waved.

Afterwards, whenever I needed a few screws or a paintbrush, I would stop by Spiros' store which was always bustling. You squeezed through rather than walked, while the other hardware stores were almost always empty. Behind the counter, one hand on the computer the other on the phone, talking to three people at once, Spiros, who only longed to be out of doors among his animals or working his vegetable garden, saw everything and everyone in the store, even the ones that stole. He never stopped them. He felt they must need it.

"Besides, they don't steal much, a few screws. Maybe a paintbrush."

He only charged customers whatever he thought they could afford. If you were struggling he would only charge his cost and then make up for it by charging retail to the English. Only later did I realize that during that time I was one of the English.

After that time at the restaurant, I saw him while I was in my jeep with Guido and he was walking up the road towards our land, boots deep in mud. I pulled up next to him and offered him a ride, which he politely refused. He didn't want to dirty my car. Not until I was insistent did he quietly accept, and as we rode the rest of the way, he scratched Guido's head and talked about how peaceful and beautiful this particular ridge was, then pointed to the sea in front of my land:

"That is where Xerxes, the Persian, and his navy first fought the Greeks. Xerxes lost many ships and his fleet had to go back and around the island on their way down to Marathon."

Across the road, near the entrance to what would become my driveway, a primitive but charming fence and gate had been recently erected on a large piece of land whose neglected acres had been cleared and olive trees cleaned in the last few weeks. Spiros explained that he had received permission from his cousin to plant four hundred and fifty grape vines on some old family land to make wine for his family and friends. Stepping out of the jeep, he took my hand.

"You and your wife must come to dinner at my house on Saturday. I have your telephone number. From the door handles. I call you." Then, as he backed away he smiled, "Call me if you need something."

Blessed with good neighbors on three sides.

On Saturday, Spiros met us on the main road and we followed him to a duplex on Achladies Beach, which he and Matoula shared with her mother, Loula, her sister, Mercini, and her two year old niece, Danae. Delighted by the invitation, Anthea and I were quite taken by the wonderful architectural details of their apartment which had been designed by Spiros, who had poured through piles of architectural books as part of his continual self education. The exquisite taste and quality of the furnishings, Matoula's contribution, were mostly Greek antiques and fabrics assembled with a wonderful sense of proportion, style, and color. We couldn't have felt more at home in such splendid surroundings and, as is custom on this island, when you make a friend you make a friend of the family, Matoula's mother, Loula, was included, and she and Matoula cooked and Spiros poured excellent wines nonstop and amazed us with his vast store of knowledge garnered from his reading everything from Proust to Chomsky.

The dinner became the first of many exquisite meals together which might include Loula's brother, Thomas, a retired sea captain, Mercini, who would bring the entertainment, delightful little Danae, and at other times upwards of thirty family and friends.

Spiros and his family became our adopted family: traditional, worldly wise yet innocent, happy, gentle yet fun loving and always so kind, and whose relatives and friends also welcomed us as their own. From the time I picked him up in my jeep, Spiros would always say upon leaving me:

"Call me if you need something."

And he always meant it. Endlessly curious, scrupulously honest, and generous to a fault, he quickly became my best friend. It was a wonderful surprise. We had much in common and were spending many hours together, most of which included the whole or part of the family. Anthea heartily approved and also enjoyed being with the women, who helped with her Greek vocabulary as they planned future dinners and exchanged recipes, and had a special fondness for Matoula, who owned the chic clothing store on the island and shared, among her other gifts, Anthea's design sensibility.

Besides building a house, we were quickly, effortlessly, merrily building a life.

SIGA SIGA

If you should put even a little on a little,
and should do this often,
soon this too would become big.

Hesiod

The day we decided to move to Greece, Anthea began pouring through books on Mediterranean architecture while I scoured the Internet for Greek island property. By the time we had decided on Skiathos, Anthea, the designer, had rough sketches of Mediterranean houses, one and two stories, hillside and flatland, just in case we decided to stay on Skiathos, and just in case we stayed and decided to buy property and we couldn't find a house and were forced to build. When she penciled in the colors, the house would, of course, be white, the shutters the pale green side of the olive leaf, and the front door the yellow of a lemon; but which lemon? After setting aside two lemons from the market, she watched as they steadily grew a richer, darker yellow before she decided on the exact shade. By the time we moved to Greece, Anthea had designed the interior rooms with floor plans that included our rugs and furniture, and elevations that included fireplace mantles, doors and windows, the design decisions being based on our possessions. Walls were designed to fit pieces of furniture, counters to fit appliances, closets to fit clothes, ad infinitum, including which picture went on what wall, always consulting with me, sometimes by teaching me, other times by listening to my needs and preferences.

Geof had introduced us to Tasoula, a local Greek woman in her early forties whom he trusted completely to be our surveyor, architect, engineer, contractor and builder, and to obtain our plans and permits quickly and efficiently. We were still in those illusive "plans and permits quickly and efficiently" stage when we had to confront the unnerving fact that it was already the end of March and the Villa Thalia was ours for only two more months. Since monthly rentals were rare because of the inflated rental prices during the summer season, we were grateful when Geof called to say that near the village by the airport, nestled amid a very old olive grove at the end of a long driveway, there was a small Greek house next to a soccer field, which the owners would be willing to rent to us for a year at a reasonable rate, since they had recently moved to a larger house they had just built.

Older Greek houses are rather small. Geof told me it was because most of the people spent their day working outside in the sun and slept in a small room with a fireplace at night. One quick look and we decided that in spite of its size, or because of it, the house was charming, and two months later we repacked our twenty boxes and were in the process of moving into the cottage when the owner, Vasilis, a tall strong Skiathan jeweller of no uncertain charm, pulled down the driveway on a shiny black motorcycle, wearing a brown suede jacket.

"It's nice, the house, eh?"

"It's great, Vasilis. But it doesn't have a toilet seat."

"I know. I took it for my new house. A nice one. Wood."

"Ah, wood. Well, could we get a toilet seat?"

"What?"

"A toilet seat. It should have a toilet seat."

"A toilet seat?" he looked at me like I was insisting he remodel the kitchen but was really wondering whether it was incumbent upon him to furnish a toilet seat to a tenant.

"You want a toilet seat?"

"The toilet doesn't have a seat" I pleaded.

"You want a toilet seat?"

"Yes, I do, Vasilis. I think the toilet should have one."

"You want a toilet seat, I'll get you a toilet seat" he sighed, the exigencies of being a landlord to spoiled Americans, "And don't worry, has big pipes."

"Oh, yes, I know, I'm very happy about that."

And I really was. The older plumbing in Greece used such narrow pipes that you couldn't put paper into the toilet but had to deposit it into a receptacle, sometimes with a lid, sitting alongside. I couldn't imagine it.

By now, it was the beginning of June and the days were growing longer by leaps and bounds, beach tavernas were opening one by one, small hotels were welcoming guests, and some of the larger beaches even had a few sun bathing tourists. Parking was becoming increasingly restricted in the village, and freshly painted kayikis, traditional shallow-hulled Greek boats, were functioning as public buses picking people up at one beach and dropping them at another or at the port in the village. A horse and carriage began running tourists up and down the quay, while on Papadiamanti Street, a veiled old lady in black with a white cane and dark glasses was in a wheel chair, holding out a tin cup, a sign hanging from her neck in English, "I am blind", and I wondered how she managed the trip over and where and how well she was rooming and how much she netted after expenses each day. Gypsies were suddenly emerging everywhere, selling everything from garden furniture to piglets out of trucks, while sidewalk vendors hawking everything from temporary tattoos to cashews appeared on the streets. In just a few weeks the changes had been astonishing. The island was quickly swelling from six to what would become sixty thousand during the next few months. Shops were unshuttered and stayed open seven days a week, from eight-thirty in the morning until midnight. Bars were opened, cars, motorbikes, boats, and rooms were being rented, garbage trucks were emptying all the trash bins every day. There were no holidays for workers as everyone seemed wedded to the season, except the tourists who came in planes from Athens, London and Hamburg, or on the ferries in buses, cars, motorcycles, or on foot, all with a smile that would last the week or two or three. Vacation! At last!

On June 15th, schools closed and children who were old enough were running errands for parents or working alongside, learning their trade. It wasn't uncommon to see a pre-teen boy travelling with his father inside a backhoe and even operating the heavy machine, or a small six year old girl weighing and pricing produce at the corner market, which was suddenly bursting with excellent locally grown fruits and vegetables. The season Greeks longed for had sadly become a grueling marathon for most of the islanders as they doggedly worked in order to make a year's income in the next twelve weeks. The air was also changing. It was becoming denser, warmer, and the sea was quickly following. Sailboats and motor yachts were replacing the small fishing boats while, closer to shore, speed boats began pulling skiers and rafts shaped like yellow bananas, which bounced wildly in their wake. Besides tavernas and boat rides, most of the popular beaches also had umbrella concessions, although on every beach there was plenty of unfettered space and there were dozens of beaches with no umbrellas or concessions and few people if any. Old fat women lounging bare breasted, children playing in the sand, young couples lazily tapping paddle balls to each other, larger groups swatting bigger balls in waist high water, bathing beauties, body building hunks, the beaches of Skiathos were becoming one large playground and wonderful people watching posts. Couples were wandering lonely dirt roads under cloudless skies, stopping in someone's orchard to pick a few cherries or a peach or plum. Others explored the smallest roads and paths on rented motorbikes, photographing breathtaking vistas.

Anthea and I wiled away the time waiting for our building plans to be approved, Anthea studying her Greek dictionary for words she needed to know and weren't part of a six year old's vocabulary, words like "molding" and "shower head". We were living a forties romantic comedy at Vasilis' cozy cottage, spending lazy evenings sitting on the porch after dinner, watching the planes thunder and roar within spitting distance overhead, shaking the table and dishes, while watching a soccer game amid several hundred screaming fans on the next lot. Then, after the soccer games, when the last fans had left and beginning just as we were falling asleep and recurring at a number of intervals during the night, a cry from one lone animal from the lot on the other side, then another, then barks and cries from several other animals, and suddenly choruses of animals, a huge barnyard of sounds, donkeys braying and sheep and goats and horses wailing and howling together with dogs and cats for an hour or more until just before dawn when, after an hour's silence, the roosters would wake the barnyard again, a whole new day. In the early mornings, I would walk to the village past the fishing boats, then up the steps to the Church of the Three Hierarchs where I would light several candles, always including one for us, then across the square to the bakery where Stamatis the baker, a red faced man with thinning hair in his late thirties, would set down his *bouzouki* and offer me an espresso to go with the reward for my walk, a sugar doughnut, Greek style, which meant larger and lighter and fresh out of the oven.

Friends came to visit as well as Robert, who announced he would be coming with a new lady friend. With this news Anthea groaned. Our history with the girls he had brought home was at best checkered. One was so shy that even after several dinners with just the four of us, she would still only speak to us through him and only by whispering in his ear:

"Could your father pass the salt?"

Then, there was a debutante from Santa Barbara in a state of extreme rebellion with multi-colored spiked hair and black nail polish and many tattoos and piercings who did talk, but endlessly, and with an attitude. A number of others followed, each odder than the last, so it was with a growing unease that we waited at the port for Robert's boat to arrive.

He emerged from the hydrofoil, looking tired and harried with a woman fifteen years his senior with a burnt orange wig. Anthea took my arm:

"Oh, dear."

At that moment, the orange lady veered off, waving, revealing a petite beauty with coal-black hair. Robert grinned when he spied us, then tapped the young lady on the shoulder and pointed. She saw me waving and smiled openly. Anthea smiled cautiously back.

The young couple spent a month of complete bliss, lolling at the beaches, dancing in the clubs and in between having long lunches and dinners and walks and talks with us. How fortunate to have a child who, as an adult, you love having dinner with! His friend, Hope, also very smart, was always cheerful and easy to be with. Originally from a rural part of California, she became a Laker Girl, part of an all female cheerleading dance squad that performed at Los Angeles Laker games all over the world. Now in her mid twenties, she was an elementary school teacher who chose to work in the Los Angeles inner city school system. We were touched by her selflessness.

We hadn't been able to spend this kind of concentrated time with Robert since he was a boy. Although he had not physically changed, he had changed. Anthea noticed it almost immediately. He seemed calmer. More authentically self-assured. More willing to engage in a more focused way about deeper subjects. Life subjects. He was a gifted writer and storyteller and had an excellent sense of style and color, and we told each other while planning our retirement that it would probably be a good thing for us not to be hovering over him while he made his way. Rather than relying on our contacts and friends, he would be compelled to forge his own life, in his own way, at his own pace. His friends, not necessarily our friends. His style, not necessarily ours. We tried to convince each other it would strengthen him, center him, clarify him. And yet, there always lingered the doubt that we had skillfully made that case in order to justify our selfish pursuit. Over the month, we were delighted to observe that both things were probably true.

The happy couple stayed in the tiny guest room, and it was fun living in the small space with them. We did our own housekeeping and had small dinner parties on the terrace, between the time the flies and wasps left for the day and before the mosquitoes arrived. It was one of those lazy nights when, after much wine, I stumbled onto the Plus One Third Rule: Everything in construction regarding time and money is underestimated by a third, no matter what it is.

"They will start on Monday" means that if Monday is three days away and you add a third, they'll start on Tuesday. If it's Monday three months from now, it'll be Tuesday four months. If it costs one 100,000 euros, it really will be 133,000, no matter what, and it wasn't anyone's fault. I was again reminded of Heraclitus who, if he had lived on Skiathos, would have included besides the air, the sea, and the earth always changing, the prices, the rules, and the schedules.

Regardless of the Plus One Third Rule, our plans of building on the land we bought were finally approved. With the great good news Anthea immediately paled. As she always did at the idea of change.

Having received permission to dig for water, Tasoula enlisted the service of Kostas, a well-digger, and Old Fotis, an ageless wisp of a man with a weathered, hollow, deep-lined face, who we all followed as he strolled down the hill, away from the building site, scooping up a bouquet of wild thyme here, a bunch of wild oregano there, in addition to four or five plants which he identified to Tasoula and put into a plastic bag.

"For digestion", Tasoula translated, "For sleeping."

From his back pocket Fotis produced an old olive branch, not unlike the slingshot of my childhood, except the branches were slightly longer. Holding it towards the ground with one hand, he stopped and started several times, then took a firm stand, gripped the handle with his other hand, and I watched stunned as the branches bent to the ground. He smiled at me, revealing an absence of molars, then turned the branch away and I could see it straightening, then back again and it bent again, and the closer he brought it to the ground the more it would bend. Worth the 20 euros just for the show. But Fotis wasn't satisfied with that spot, and he continued picking greens and stopping, pointing, bending, until finally, after about a half hour, he went back and dropped the branch on a spot I was sure he had dismissed twenty minutes before.

"That's the spot!" announced Tasoula.

"I'll begin in three days!" declared Kostas.

Back then, I hadn't yet formulated the Plus One Third Rule so, of course, Guido and silly me waited in vain for Kostas on the third day from seven in the morning until four in the afternoon. But I didn't mind. I knew Anthea would be happy back at the cottage, drawing details of fireplaces and doors, or looking through our clothes for the perfect wall and fabric colors. I had already lost one of my favorite sweatshirts because it was the color of the office ceiling and if I wore it, we would have to wash it and it would become a different shade. But I was happy just to be there, sitting under an olive tree, watching the hydrofoils inch by on the distant sea, and the big merchant ships which moved so slowly they seemed to be standing still, ships crewed by Philippinos and North Africans, doing what Greeks did a generation ago, back-breaking work, sending money home, watching their children grow from a distance and knowing their labor was quite often what stood between their loved ones and inescapable poverty. Seeing them was always humbling, a reminder of my own lazy, privileged life, a man who for the most part played for a living. Not a star, just a Hollywood film actor, well paid to arrive on a film set in the early morning where someone would shave me while I slept in a makeup chair, and someone else would bring me a hot breakfast of my choosing while I lay in my dressing room, reading, watching television or napping, waiting for a camera rehearsal when I would pretend to be a gangster or a cop for a few minutes, then retire to my room and wait for lunch.

From the morning I first saw that little piece of Greece, I visited the land with its old stone retaining walls at least twice every day, walking the land with Guido, or reclining under one of the trees, listening to the goat bells clinking through the pines, imagining. I enjoyed it so much, I even persuaded Anthea to join us one perfect sunny afternoon for a picnic. The Brooklyn girl had never been on a picnic except once in her living room and couldn't imagine why anyone would want to eat out in a field without a table and a chair, but she reluctantly agreed. She packed provisions for twelve: olives, two kinds of pickles, potato sticks, cold chicken, salami, mustard, mayonnaise, potato and tomato salad, green salad, several cheeses, hard boiled eggs, bread, fruits, nuts, raisins, water, wine, plates, silver, napkins, a blanket.

"This ground is so hard."

I was unpacking, "Sit over here. I think it's softer."

Anthea was moving to the other side of the blanket, arranging the food and setting the table.

"I think something just bit me."

"Where?"

"On my leg. Can you see it?"

"Where???"

"There, what are you, blind?"

"I don't see anything."

"I'm not really hungry."

After waiting in vain for Kostas on the fourth day until five o'clock, Guido and I gave up and went back to the cottage. Later that day, Kostas drove his drilling rig to the sight and shored it up with rocks and boards. He had begun. The next morning around ten, another truck appeared carrying drill bits and shafts, and Kostas stepped out, big and square in his wide shorts and big belly:

"*Kalimera!*"

Without another word, he and a younger assistant went directly to work, unloading heavy iron bits and shafts for the next thirty minutes. After that, they stopped and took what I would soon realize was the island's customary morning instant Nescafé Frappé break: instant coffee powder to which the two added water and shook vigorously, then they sat and smoked, and talked and laughed for another twenty minutes. According to a survey by the European Union, Greeks ate more, drank more, smoked more, and were more overweight than any other people in the European Union, yet they lived the longest, all due to lack of stress. *Siga siga*, a favorite Greek expression which means slowly slowly, was a characteristic in Anthea that I was aware of because she moved at twenty-five miles an hour while I moved at sixty. But I was unaware it was a national trait. Slowly slowly, Kostas worked, yet like Anthea, with a clarity and certainty that more than made up for the lack of speed. Today was unloading. Tomorrow he would drill and the ground would belch brown, and then in two more days, at forty-five meters, Kostas would hit granite and the hole would spew white powder and chips, until at eighty-five meters he would hit water, a gusher, and continue drilling for another thirty-five meters for good measure. After allowing clear water to gush for a half hour, Kostas took a sample for me to take to the laboratory for testing. In two days we had our answer.

"So clean and salt and iron free, with a simple mud filter you could bottle and sell it."

If I ever saw Old Fotis again, I might have hugged him. Few things ever thrilled or comforted me more than knowing I had my own clean water supply, and that no matter what, we could survive. I was living a life more carefree than I could ever remember, a life without debt, yet with a personal water source and fruit bearing olive, fig, pear and chestnut trees and land that would grow most vegetables. I was ready for World War III so long as it wasn't nuclear and didn't involve Greece. I don't think Anthea was nearly as thrilled or comforted by the notion.

Many couples don't survive the building process. For us, it was not a problem. For the first fifteen years of our living together, at least once a month, Anthea and I would have such a fight that we would decide to split up and divide the furniture.

"I want the desk!"

"You take the goddamn desk, I'm taking the armoire!"

Until the day when, in the middle of dividing the furniture, the phone rang. It was my agent. Would I want to go to Australia for two weeks? Neither of us had ever been to Australia. I looked at her while I put my agent on hold.

"You want to go to Australia for two weeks?"

She looked at me strangely, realizing, just as I had in that moment, that we were never really going to divide the furniture, that all the fights over the last fifteen years were really hollow, then she nodded with her hazel eyes as close to tears as I'd ever seen. We went to Australia together and never fought again. But we argued. Sometimes endlessly.

A friend reminded me of an evening she spent with us several years ago in our kitchen in Hollywood, sitting across from Anthea's brother, Thom, who was reading aloud from a book on the history of vegetables, while Anthea and I were standing at either end of the table, screaming at each other about which culture contributed more to Western civilization, the Greeks or the Arabs. She said the scene was oddly unalarming, and at no stage had the fight become personal.

Building was waiting. Waiting for the workmen to finish another job. Waiting for them to arrive. Waiting for a day when it didn't rain. Waiting for material from Volos, Skiathos' lifeline to the mainland. Waiting for a delivery. Waiting for a part, a tool, a man to pee. It was totally maddening, but with every milestone - the building pad, the foundation, the posts, a ceiling - there was the thrill of seeing your own creation evolving; and Tasoula, our black-haired little general, always on her cell phone, driving the crew to work in her junk yard truck bouncing up the dirt road, grinning, thinking, her beautiful blonde seven year old daughter, Filaretti, wandering in the field with Guido, picking flowers. It was a splendid time.

"What? Everyone is taking off the whole month of August? They always do? Oh, well, *siga siga*."

Guido and I would arrive in the morning with the workmen, whether they showed or not, and stay until the workmen left. Close enough to see but far enough to leave them alone, I would pretend to be thinking important thoughts. It took each new crew a few days to realize I was there to watch and learn. I was fascinated by their skills whether driving a bulldozer or hammering a nail, and their ingenuity, their ability to create tools on the spot, using available materials. How many uses for a plastic water bottle! This man's waste became that man's material. And the camaraderie among the workers. There was always one clown while the leader was the straight man and usually the two were good friends if not relatives, and it was all in fun and the work was getting done *siga siga*, but surely.

Late in the summer, we began to notice Guido coughing as if trying to clear his throat. We didn't think anything of it at first, but when it seemed to be getting worse, we were convinced he possibly had something caught. Guido had been with us for nine years. I picked him out, the handsomest and most frolicking of the litter. We had decided to get a companion for our other black standard poodle, Max, a five year old, who seemed to appear so lonely whenever we drove away from the house in Hollywood. But Max developed colitis the day Guido arrived and spent the rest of his life hiding from him in closets and under beds, even when he was too old to run and Guido was ministering to him.

Guido was a beautiful animal, elegant, smart, wondrously athletic. Completely untrained by us, he learned by watching Max. So polite he wouldn't cross the threshold to the bedroom until he was invited. Originally, I wanted to call him Guido because, although we lived in Thorny's house and the lot was surrounded by a high fence and gates and we had an alarm system, a private police force, a thirty-eight revolver filled with buckshot in my nightstand drawer and a large dog, we still didn't feel safe, and I thought if a burglar broke in downstairs while we were sleeping, I would be able to yell in my best gangster voice.

"Max! Guido!"

And the sound of many feet on the steps and dogs barking might scare a robber away. And now Guido, always warm and playful, who had been my constant companion since he was twelve weeks old, was trying to cough up something stuck in his throat, and Yiannis, the veterinarian on the island, felt a lump and said it might be cancer and we should get an x-ray from the vet in Volos, who showed us the x-ray and said there was nothing he could do, and the head veterinarian at the College of Veterinary Medicine in Thessalonika agreed, and all the while that thing stuck in his throat was getting bigger and bigger and he could only eat tiny bits at a time, until he couldn't eat at all, or drink; and Anthea prepared his carrying case and lined it with a handsome blanket and we put Guido to sleep under his favorite pine tree. Tasoula was sobbing while one of her crew solemnly dug the hole.

In the early fall, it rained for seven straight days. No one showed at the building site but me, alone. The floors had been poured, so I could sit in an old plastic chair in what would eventually be our living room and look out over the rolling hills below and watch the sky, waiting for the rain to stop and the road to dry out enough to allow the trucks to pass, so they could continue delivering materials. It gave me time to look back at the distance I had travelled in the last months, a distance I would never have imagined had I not given myself permission, the key to any dream coming true. And this part of the dream was finally taking shape, double brick walls with insulation, and with every wall I would get more of the sense of a particular room, and then room to room, knowing where the furniture would be and the view from my side of the bed. For almost a whole year, day after day, it would become my life, watching each brick and nail, each splash of plaster and snip of wire, and when the men had left for the day, I would stay and walk the floors, imagining.

"Come in, please. Into the hallway, here. Now, step into the living room. Yes, it is spacious."

And then, one day, the electric company was digging holes for the sixteen poles which would carry our wire to the main terminal, and the wires were hung, and for the first time I realized that I had marred the natural beauty of the country road through the old olive groves. I felt slightly ashamed. Man had entered the forest. Then the telephone company arrived with their sixteen poles and their lines. Why can't we all share the same poles! But my shame soon evaporated with the pleasure of now being able to be up at the house at night with a lamp, and then a second, which I would plug in and sit by the phone and dream and look out over the sea. The full moon lighted the sea and countryside so brightly you could read a book. The absence of the moon would reveal a shower of stars, the kind that I had only read about in books. Sitting listening to the sound of the cicadas, gazing down at the lights from the small settlement by the sea, watching the occasional boat's running lights disappear in the distance, as calming as it was, it also encouraged a growing impatience, like a child anticipating the arrival of Santa Claus: I could hardly wait to be living there.

Tasoula's husband, Stamatis, was now around more and more. He looked like my father in his late forties, but with red hair. The Maestro, he was called, especially sarcastically by his wiry thin gap toothed assistant, Eleftherios, because he could do anything in any building department, and skillfully. With a confidence that extended to taste and style as well, he was always greatly amused by our aesthetic choices. When Anthea told him she wanted to paint some of the interior walls a dove grey he stopped working and looked at her as if she was asking him to commit a crime.

"Why not white? When they asked Picasso what color he wanted to paint his house he answered 'Why not white?'"

Several days after the walls had been painted, he confessed to Tasoula he wanted to paint their walls dove grey.

"Because you don't have to repaint them every year."

There was a group of Albanian men in Skiathos who were constantly lending each other money to keep each other afloat, and who stood at the same spot at the edge of the village every morning until nine o'clock, hoping to get a day's work often enough to allow them to stay on Skiathos and perhaps even climb another rung up the ladder by finding permanent work. Aliens from the poorest country in Europe, I would see them every morning on my way to our land.

"Try not to run over any Albanians riding a motorbike."

"What? Why?"

"Because it might be your motorbike!"

I heard the joke twice my first week on Skiathos. Of course, one could easily have substituted Greeks in the United States a generation ago.

One of the Albanians who found semi permanent labor on Skiathos was Nikos who, at fifteen, walked alone from his village in Albania, down and across Greece, and finally to the ferry which would take him to the island in order to find work to make enough money to go back to Albania and start a small business. Nikos had been helping build our house. There was as much of him in those walls and floors as anybody. Under a mop of curly rust colored prematurely thinning hair, he would be standing in the bed of Tasoula's old truck every morning and at the end of every day. He dug Guido's grave. Whenever there was any hard labor to be done, he was the designated hand. Working steadily, evenly, with a strong determination, nothing was too hard, nothing could wear down his lean twenty-eight year old body. He would be left alone working on the property in the hottest summer sun, shirtless with heavy work pants and thick leather boots, pouring sweat while digging a dusty deep trench, first with a pick, then with a shovel, breaking up the rocky soil and piling it to one side where he would shovel it back on yet another sizzling summer day. Or I would see him in the coldest part of winter, with bare hands shoveling cement and stones into a mixer, sweat having turned to ice in his hair, behind him a twenty gallon tin can with air holes where a fire was burning discarded ends of board and olive branches, trying to warm his small hemisphere. With no personal agenda to distract me, I had the time to see the whole of his life, not simply how it affected my life, and me, and it made me examine my part in his burden. The quiet appreciation in his eyes for any small kindness I might offer, a hot tea, a small bottle of cool water drunk in seconds, a cold beer at the end of the day, even a "*Kalimera*" on the street, although I rarely saw him on the street since he worked seven days a week as often as he could, where and whenever he could, sending money home, counting the humiliations until he could be back in Albania with his own business and some small dignity. He was proud to be Albanian, and especially sensitive to any slight, but was obligated to hold his temper when those like Stamatis made jokes about the intelligence of Albanians. As with any day laborer, there was little job security, and as an alien there was even less. Still, he was one of the luckier, finding steady work with Tasoula, and as the months slowly went by for him it seemed every day he lost another pound until he was pure muscle, skin and bone. I grew to trust him completely and once asked him if, when our house was finished and we were away for a while, he would stay in it and I would pay him. He said he'd rather not stay there, but he would come up every day and look after the house for nothing.

One of the men who had dug our swimming pool at the Thornberry house in Hollywood was one of the Step Brothers, a famous black tap-dance brother act. Even though they had a star on Hollywood Boulevard, the act was now old history and he was seventy-something and reduced to digging pools to supplement his meager social security, a lesson in the truth about the ladder of success going both ways. A man of uncommon dignity he didn't seem to resent having fallen so low, but instead was proud and told stories and showed clippings of their once very popular act, grateful for the success he had enjoyed. He worked at a slow but steady pace, every few minutes stopping to allow himself an important luxury, one very large Cuban cigar a day which he would light in the morning and smoke intermittently the rest of the day, wrapping the butt in a leaf and putting it carefully in his pocket when he left.

Before making a living in film and television, I had a litany
of jobs after the leather factory: school bus driver, substitute
teacher, waiter in a Mafia godfather's restaurant, bouncer in
a Lesbian bar, drummer in a female impersonator review,
tuna and egg salad maker for a large drugstore chain's lunch
counters, parking lot concession owner for two strip joints,
to name just a few, all good experiences for a young character
actor or even for an older man currently retired, whose future
was by no means assured. Much of the economic freedom
we enjoyed depended on the integrity of our pensions and
the strength of the dollar, which didn't seem to be based on
much beyond habit, and in fact had lost over thirty percent
of its value against the euro in the short time we had been
in Greece. Somewhere in the back of my mind, no matter
how blissful my life, I knew there was another side out there
and possibly waiting, for as Solon said, "Often enough the
Gods give a man a glimpse of happiness, and then utterly ruin
him." We had no plan B. It was just us. No fortune or safety
net waiting from family, and the further you strayed from
Hollywood, the sooner you were forgotten, not because of
bridges burned, but because the cast of characters changed so
quickly and the new ones weren't really interested in the old
ones. What would we do? We were alone at sea. I never had
to do hard physical labor. What could we do was one of the
questions haunting me as I watched our house take shape. We
were somewhere in the middle of the ladder and I couldn't
help keeping my eye on both the rung above and the one below, especially below, because fortune can change at any moment and you can't consider yourself well settled until you're
dead, just lucky. Always lurking was the suspicion that Solon
was speaking directly to me and it frightened me because I
couldn't imagine I would have the strength like Nikos or the
Step Brother, both of whom I admired so much for their will,
their clarity, and their integrity, to accept without bitterness

whatever circumstance they might be in. It seems nothing is so unsettling as knowing you'll never be settled until you're dead.

The Plus One Third Rule is not without exception. On rare occasions, it could turn out to be the Minus One Half Exception. In our case, having discussed the move-in date with Tasoula so that we could coordinate the shipping date for the furniture from California, the shipment arrived two months early and was sitting under a baking sun on a pier in Piraeus, the port of Athens. Tasoula suggested we take delivery and put it on our terrace covered in plastic sheets, but Anthea didn't warm to the idea of our antique French country furniture sitting in the dirt under a plastic wrap outside a construction site for eight weeks, so we arranged to have it stored.

We were now in that stage of building where I had to watch everyone very carefully; silly things, like making sure the electrician set every plug and light switch in the room the same distance from the floor, and convincing the plumber that somewhere in his system was a leak because there was water on the hardwood floor. Then, there were the hurried calls to Anthea to rush up and have a conversation with the carpenter who was in love and so mismeasured all the cabinets and needed her to modify her molding design. Radiators and toilets and sinks were being delivered, many absent essential parts, tiles were being laid, floors sanded, re-sanded, then sanded again, and all the while, although I pretended to be calm and understanding, my impatience continued to grow. As move-in day approached, we also became increasingly concerned about the daunting task of keeping the ark clean because the most reliable cleaning help on the island worked in the hotels in the summer and were only available in the winter months. Tasoula said she didn't know anyone but would find someone to come by and wash the walls and floors during the move.

The morning of the move, while I paced the floor and
Stamatis and Eleftherios were still hammering in floor molding
and the painter was still painting the doors, in strode Maria, a
handsome, strapping woman with a mop of short tight curls,
who looked like my aunt Josephine at forty. She was catching
wasps with her bare hand and throwing them out the door,
while ordering Stamatis to wipe his feet as she washed and
wiped the windows. Anthea begged for this miracle to continue to work for us, to which she agreed for two days a week
- a sign that it was going to be a great day.

At noon, I first saw the two moving vans filled with our
furniture lumbering up the dirt road to our house. In addition,
I had bought a small used black lacquer Russian baby grand
piano in Athens months before, whereupon, after refinishing
and refurbishing it, the company had agreed to deliver it to my
door in Skiathos on any given date. The piano was supposed to
have been delivered three days before, but it had been held up
leaving Athens and then again at the port, because there were
no boats that day due to the weather. Once again, I had forgotten the Plus One Third Rule, because ten days ago the piano
company promised me the piano in a week, and now inching
up the road a few meters behind the moving trucks was a rick-
ety old three wheel lorry with my precious baby grand held
down by thin ropes swaying in the back.

The two piano movers, one a small and flimsy boy, helped
the furniture movers as if they'd already planned to meet each
other, and when they had finished and moved their vans out of
the way, four of them struggled taking the piano off the truck
and the six carried it into the living room, where everyone
watched in great anticipation as Stamatis carefully uncrated it
and laid the pieces on a blanket on the floor. Cue the son of
the owner of the piano company in Athens who arrived in a
taxi, assembled and tuned the piano and then played a few

measures of different classical pieces, as Tasoula passed around an almond cake she had made from her grandmother's recipe:

"A tradition in Greece when you move in, to sweeten the house."

Although boxes were piled everywhere and all our furniture was still wrapped in plastic, it was like a reunion with old friends, and as Anthea and I ate a piece of almond cake with our fingers, we looked at each other across the room, nearly overwhelmed by the sound of the piano in our new home and the view through the clean windows and glass doors which looked like wonderful framed landscape paintings. The phones were working and all the lights were on and, as the piano tuner settled in and began playing a spirited Bach Two-Part Invention, we began laughing softly to each other, tickled that after seventeen months we two freedom lovers would be happy to have the sweet burden of home ownership again.

THE EVIL EYE

*It is the gods' custom
to bring low all things of surpassing greatness.*

Herodotus

Maria quickly took command of our new house, and on Wednesday and Saturday mornings she would wait on a bench at the town cemetery, chatting with friends, waiting for *Kyrios* Ritzid, Mister Richard, which was how she referred to me, to pick her up in the jeep at nine o'clock. After a cool *"Kalimera"*, she would sit stiffly, hands folded in her lap, barely glancing at me, quickly crossing herself three times when passing the small churches and shrines as I drove silently back up the mountain. But she always greeted Anthea with a loose grin and a wry comment which made Anthea laugh, and they would chit chat in Greek as Maria changed her shoes and gathered her cleaning things, and then they'd gossip for another ten like girlfriends before Maria began her day.

"You should have drapes with swags on the windows! An elegant villa should have drapes!"

Born in Albania of Greek parents, Maria was never without an opinion, especially when not asked, and was not shy about suggestions both practical and aesthetic. But whenever she suggested something Anthea didn't like or want, rather than tell her she didn't think it was a good idea, Anthea would blame it on me.

"*Kyrios* Ritzid doesn't want drapes. He likes to see the sea."

"Well, talk to him!"

"You talk to him."

And since *Kyrios* Ritzid didn't speak Greek and Maria couldn't speak English, the matter was well settled and, at 2:30, this vulgar and tasteless bully drove Maria back to the cemetery without a spoken word from either. And at that juncture, twice a week as I pulled to a stop outside the cemetery, as a way of showing friendship and appreciation, as a challenge to my ability to charm, even as an acting exercise, I would try to establish for even one second a personal connection with Maria, a moment of humanity by way of a warm, "*Efharisto*, Maria, *yiasou*", thank you and health. But she would never even glance at me as she returned her "*Yiasou*", fluttering her fingers goodbye, then stepped out of the jeep and strode away - if only she could speak English, she'd tell me about the drapes. But in those six hours, twice a week, Maria changed the bed sheets, mopped and vacuumed all the floors, cleaned the toilets and bathrooms, washed all the windows inside and some days outside as well, washed two and sometimes three loads of laundry, and ironed everything including underwear and sheets, even towels, dusted every little thing, kept the silver frames which covered the piano polished, picked and changed the flowers on the dining table and living room coffee table, hosed off the terrace, and took a hammer and nails and repaired any of our antique furniture that needed to be restored. In short, a superb woman of uncommon good sense, creativity, and industry who, if born into better circumstances, might today have been a bull dog of an executive in a large corporation. Instead, she was reduced to being the chief operating officer of the "Villa Anthoula", which she herself named using the diminutive of Anthea's name, which meant "little flower", and which was how Anthea was addressed by all the Greeks on the island.

Sternly supervising any worker on the property, Maria had become an increasingly important part of our new life, constantly

on the prowl for problems in the house which needed to be addressed, like when the very hot Saturday afternoon our brand
new refrigerator broke. It was Maria who announced that the
reason was because someone who was jealous of the automatic
ice maker must have given it the evil eye.

My mother occasionally joked about an evil eye, but the
term dropped out of my life until I met Anthea who, whenever
she or anyone she liked received a compliment, would quickly
spit three times and say under her breath in Greek, "*Skortha sta
matia sou*", Garlic in your eyes. When someone she happened
not to like received a compliment, she always smiled, which I
used to think was elegant of her, before I understood she wasn't
exactly being generous. The evil eye is given by someone, even
unknowingly, who is jealous of you or your possession. You
could even give yourself the evil eye by gloating or admiring
yourself or one of your things.

Maria immediately filled a tall glass of water and grabbed
the bottle of olive oil, while Anthea described the test for the
evil eye.

"If the oil stays on top of the water, which is where it usually
does, there is no evil eye. But if it goes to the bottom, that's
the test."

I watched amused as Maria poured a glob of oil onto the
water. Immediately the oil plopped to the bottom of the glass
in two big blobs. After many signs of the cross and a few exple-
tives, Maria explained that this was very bad and definitely the
reason for the refrigerator crashing and did we know anyone
with blue eyes, because people with blue eyes can give the evil
eye easier than brown eyed people. I knew a few people with
blue eyes, but I didn't know what to believe. It sounded too
much like one of those things she told Anthea from time to
time, like if it rained on the bride's wedding day she was going to be fat, or if she ate a clove of garlic every morning in
April she wouldn't have a cold all year. Although it was true

that anyone on the island who saw the refrigerator's ice and filtered cold water window, which we took for granted, seemed to admire it. And a few of them did have blue eyes. Years ago, when I was parking cars in Hollywood, a friend took me to see a psychic who told me things about myself and my childhood which astonished me. When I started writing her a check for which I had no funds, she gently put her hand on mine and smiled knowingly:

"You can pay me next time."

Which I soon did. Hollywood was filled with psychics, and after that reading I became fascinated by the idea that the future was actually knowable. One woman even predicted that I would buy the Camino Palmero house when I was already in escrow on a Mediterranean house in another part of town. Insisting she saw the house, she described it in some detail including a lap pool. A month later, the owner of the Mediterranean house changed their mind about selling and, after suing them and being advised after a year that the outcome couldn't be guaranteed, I decided to look for another. Not remembering the prophecy, I saw the Camino Palmero house and bought it. It didn't have a pool. A year later, having built a lap pool, I saw her again and she reminded me of the reading. At the house, I found the cassette she had provided at the time. Not only did she describe the house perfectly, she also mentioned stepping down to the lap pool a few steps below.

Some psychics believed they were getting impressions from an intelligent universe, which knew all. Some thought they were only reading your subconscious, which inexplicably held your future as well as your past. Try as I might, I could never explain the phenomenon. The more I investigated, the more mysterious the world became. Life was governed by numbers, planets, birthdays. Unseen sources directed or instructed through cards, bones, tea leaves, and coffee grounds. Karmic vibrations endlessly rolled through the universe, the dead communicated with the living, sometimes even through reincarnated children, not to mention ghosts, possessions, and strange people with healing powers. I was even one of twelve guests gathered in someone's living room in Beverly Hills one day and told by our host who called himself Bo, and our hostess, who called herself Peep, that they were the archangels Michael and Gabriel and we twelve were the reincarnated Apostles of Christ and should leave our possessions and follow them to a waiting spaceship in Oregon to meet our master in heaven. That was the day I decided to leave the metaphysical mysteries for others to plumb.

Anthea, who never believed in psychic phenomena, was nonetheless superstitious, a piece of *Yiayia* Maria she carried with her. Her grandmother, whenever anyone became ill, did the same test, but if the oil went to the bottom, they called the priest because the patient had the evil eye and couldn't be cured by a doctor. If it stayed on top, they would call the doctor.

To ward off the curse, we needed eyes of our own which were for sale in the village in many different sizes in glass, plaster, tin, and stone, always with a blue iris. The eye is then hung on a string, nailed on a wall, worn as a pin, ring, or earring, and placed in strategic sites around the home or person. I still didn't know what to believe, so I did nothing. Besides, the electrician told us it was because the power was surging and we needed surge protectors. Why he neglected to warn us before we bought all new appliances I leave to wiser men to fathom, but we contacted the dealer who made us aware that to have it repaired and still maintain the warranty, we would have to have the official factory representative on Skiathos do the work.

All weekend we kept the refrigerator door closed to try and save drawers full of cheeses and meats I had bought earlier in the day, and on Monday, at nine o'clock, I called Yiorgos, the official factory representative, but his cell phone was out of range and there was no message service. I called two hours later. Same. Then after lunch, same. I called Tuesday morning. He answered briskly. He spoke English quite well, so I explained our refrigerator wasn't working and it was still under warranty and I had just bought drawers of meats and cheeses. He understood perfectly and said he would be right up.

Feeling slightly relieved, I slipped open the fridge and picked out a bottle of warm milk and made myself my morning oatmeal. After a half hour without any sign of Yiorgos, I assumed he had gotten lost and I called him on his cell phone. No answer. I exited the house and walked down the driveway looking for a sign. Nothing. Returning to the house I called again, no answer. I called again before lunch, once again after lunch, then in the middle of the afternoon and again just before dinner. I was hoping nothing had happened to him, and not just because he was the only official factory representative on the island.

Wednesday morning I called again. He answered. Upon hearing my voice he apologized profusely but there was an emergency in a hotel he had to take care of because it affected so many people, and he was very busy today but he'd be up by five o'clock.

At noon, Anthea and I, aggravated, cleaned out the refrigerator which smelled of stinking cheese and rotten meat and vegetables. At five o'clock, I stepped outside to wait for Yiorgos. At six, I stepped back inside and called. No answer.

The ugly American would have a few words to say to this factory representative when he finally showed. But it would not be that night or even the next day or the next. His phone was once again out of range for the next several days and, when he finally did answer, he apologized profusely but had to rush to Athens for a factory representative tutorial on another company's appliance which just happened to be our dishwasher, so I bit my tongue and begged him to come and look at our refrigerator since we had now been without one for a week during a heat wave, and I was buying ice from the grocery store,

and we were dying living out of a small cooler which would
house one small piece of meat or chicken and a few vegetables.
He seemed to sympathize and said he was coming right up.

"Ten minutes."

In an hour I called again.

"I'm on my way!" he protested.

It was late in the afternoon when the sound of a motorbike
woke me from my fit of anger. Yiorgos, a pudgy man in his
mid thirties with wild black hair, had arrived and quickly took
command of the situation.

"Do you have a screwdriver?"

Wondering just where he fit in the hierarchy of being, I watched
as Yiorgos, using our owner's manual as a reference, unscrewed
the back of the appliance and tinkered about for a minute, then
took a can of Freon out of a small case, attached it to a line and
pumped. Before long, the fridge was getting cooler and cooler,
and Yiorgos, while screwing in the back of the appliance, patiently explained how many of these new units weren't suffi-
ciently supplied with Freon and that he would complain to the
company. Then, we signed his book, entitling him to receive
compensation from the company for the visit and, although I
disliked him intensely, I warmly thanked him, shook his hand,
and walked him back to his motorbike, retrieving my screwdriver just before he drove off.

Anthea and I were grateful to have refrigeration again, so
we went out and bought many meats and cheeses and stuffed
them inside the shelves, but as Anthea was about to make dinner I checked the appliance and it seemed like the temperature
had risen again. Anthea looked at me sideways. I immediately
called Yiorgos.

"It's nothing. Just keep the door closed until tomorrow
morning to give it a chance to really get cold."

That night we went out for dinner again and prayed silently

that Yiorgos was right, that in the morning when I opened the refrigerator door, I would be greeted by a rush of arctic air.

At 7:00 a.m., snaking my hand inside the door to grab my quart of milk, I became aware that the milk was slightly above room temperature. I dialed Yiorgos.

"Don't worry, sometimes it takes a little longer. Keep it closed until noon, and if it still doesn't get cold, call me."

At noon, when it still wasn't cold, I called again, but there was no answer. I called again after lunch, just before dinner, after dinner. I was livid. Yiorgos was becoming the ultimate stress test. The meat once again had spoiled. Once again we'd have to eat out. Once again I'd have to take the little cooler to the grocery store and fill it with ice, and being people who drank wine with ice in the middle of winter, we were becoming increasingly frustrated by the inability to keep anything cold for more than an hour. It was time to go over Yiorgos' head. I called the distributor and explained my frustration. He sympathized, apologizing profusely, and said he would call Yiorgos himself and make sure he would be at my house before the end of the day. "Aha! It's true everywhere!" I called to Anthea who was sitting in front of a fan in the living room. "The squeaky wheel gets the oil!"

When Yiorgos didn't show, I called the distributor again but he had left for the day, and he wasn't in the office the following day, and wouldn't be back until Monday. So I called Yiorgos.

"It still doesn't get cold? I don't understand it. I'll be up in the morning, I have a very busy day today."

By now I was getting smart. In the morning, at 8:00, I called Yiorgos to remind him, but his phone was turned off. I called again at 9:00, still turned off. I continued calling every hour until 4:00 when his phone was out of range, at 5:00 when it was busy, and at six when his mother answered:

"I am in the car. Yiorgos is outside picking salad greens for supper. I'll have him call you."

At seven, his phone was once again turned off. By now we had been without a refrigerator for two weeks, I couldn't get Yiorgos or the distributor on the phone, and I wanted to cut Yiorgos up in little pieces and serve him with fava beans to the distributor, so I called the home office of the appliance, steaming, and asked to speak to a customer service representative.

"I understand your problem, sir, but we have difficulty getting good service people on the islands. If you want to send the refrigerator to Athens, we will have the work done free of charge but you'll have to pay for the shipping and crating."

"Thank you very much", I felt like crying.

Two days later, in the depths of despair, a familiar sound of a motorbike coming up the driveway. It was the only official factory representative in Skiathos. The distributor had called him and they had discussed the problem and it was something simple.

"You see", Yiorgos explained, "these companies keep changing the models every year, it's impossible to keep up with all the changes and this company hasn't had me come to Athens in three years. How am I supposed to keep up?"

The problem evidently wasn't the Freon, but a small part he happened to have in stock and he quickly replaced it and cautioned us not to open the door for twenty-four hours. Which we didn't. And yet, the temperature never changed. A flurry of calls in the next three days to both Yiorgos and the distributor, before I finally reached Yiorgos, who said the distributor was sending a new part, but it had to be shipped from England, and it wouldn't arrive in Athens for a week and on Skiathos for a few days after that. This part was certain to take care of the problem.

"I promise."

I wanted to bomb his store.

It took the better part of three weeks before the part was on the island and another four days before Yiorgos appeared on his motorbike. The part looked simple enough, yet complicated enough to shut down the appliance, and Yiorgos cautioned us once again about opening the door for twenty-four hours. Which we didn't, and still nothing changed. We were despondent. Yiorgos couldn't explain it. The distributor couldn't explain it. The factory couldn't explain it.

We had no choice but to ship the appliance to Athens where, if they couldn't fix it immediately, they promised to send us a brand new appliance. So Yiorgos organized two men to come in a small three wheel lorry, who wrapped blankets around the appliance, banged the wall and door frame, denting the appliance and leaving a chunk of plaster and a slice of wood missing from our house, before they managed to stand the refrigerator upright on their little truck bed, secure it with three small ropes, and rumble off down the dirt road, where it would be the last time I would ever see that pathetic failure of an appliance.

In between the time, our electrician ordered surge protectors for all our appliances and the time they were delivered and installed, our television crashed, ditto our answering machine, so, even though I still didn't quite believe, we went out and bought a dozen blue eyes which we placed in the house and car.

The morning after the surge protectors arrived and we had hung various evil eyes around our house and car, we were walking along the port to get the Herald Tribune when, while passing a refurbished automobile ferry, the Paschalis, we stopped to watch Papa Yiorgos, pastor of the Church of the Three Hierarchs, a Dustin Hoffman doppelganger with a long white beard and twinkling blue eyes, as he stood on the deck waving his censor over a make shift altar, trying to make his incantations audible above the wind. The owners were holding this blessing to introduce the old boat and its new service to the community, and many people had come and were having mezethes and drinks and toasting the new ferry.

Later, they would discover that it took the Paschalis eight hours to go from here to Volos, while it took its competitor only three. So regardless of the blessing, after six months, the Paschalis left Skiathos to be blessed somewhere else. But on that morning, Anthea, still not satisfied that our home was secure, decided she wanted a blessing for our house and she wanted Dustin Hoffman to perform the service.

Papa Yiorgos son-in-law, Kostas, drove the priest over the dusty road to our door, where he entered stroking his long beard, carrying a small leather bag which he set on a chair in the living room. Kostas had earlier advised us to set a small table with a linen cloth, a bowl of water, incense and a candle, and Papa Yiorgos covered the table with a sacred cloth, lit the incense and the candle, and proceeded with his incantations and ablutions.

I had often seen the old priest shuffling down Papadiamanti Street in his black cassock, nodding and smiling to parishioners as they kissed his hand. Husband to Calliope, father of four, a rock of constancy in Skiathos, he seemed to have it all: a nice home, a nice family, respect of the community, job security. Yet, he worked hard. Besides having to continually appear respectable, he worked all sorts of hours, saying prayers, blessing things like the Paschalis and our house.

Often, he would be up in the middle of the night, having just finished or just begun a service in his or one of the other sixty churches on the island, not to mention individual blessings and church business and raising the children and being a husband and always smiling. He figured it out for himself. Just as Hugh Hefner with his six blonde girlfriends figured it out for himself. Papa Yiorgos had the life he always dreamed of and, in addition, was assured a good place in the next.

His middle son, Nikolaos, with thick black hair and a close cropped beard and small pony tail, obviously saw his father's smile and wanted that for himself as well. He followed in his footsteps and, on almost every church occasion, he worked with his father, senior and junior priests, then walked home with him to the compound that housed most of the family and was fronted by a taverna which we frequented, En Plo, owned by his son-in-law, Kostas, and his beautiful wife, Voula, who was also the dessert chef and the old priest's only daughter. A beatific life on a small island.

As I watched him swing his censor in our living room, I was reminded of my first grade teacher, Sister Mark, who told us that any baptized Catholic could baptize anyone else and they would be saved. So I took an empty refrigerator box, two candles, a bowl of water and a crucifix and made a church where I proceeded to baptize every child in the neighborhood for a penny, because after all, every church passed a basket. At that time, I wanted to be a priest, but so many decisions in life are not made by you but for you, and although my father always said he would be proud to have one of his sons become a priest, somehow he had all six of us earmarked for something else. I was to be a lawyer, although in my high school yearbook it said I wanted to be a dentist. I must have been joking.

Papa Yiorgos concentrated on his prayer, eyes closed, and I watched more amused than prayerful as Anthea and Kostas, heads lowered, hands clasped, stood reverentially by, when I began to sense the energy in the room noticeably change. It was becoming remarkably lighter, warmer, more enveloping, more reassuring, more peaceful, even blessed.

I was awed by it, and as the feeling deepened and the realization swept through me, Papa Yiorgos opened his eyes and looked over at me and smiled. I smiled back, embarrassed that I had been looking down on the man when I clearly should have been looking up, feeling like an inchworm crawling along the sand by the sea, who has no idea there is a sea or a bird or even a flower, wondering just exactly where I belonged in the hierarchy of being.

Two months after our refrigerator disappeared on the back

of the little lorry, having made flurries of calls to the factory, the distributor, and to Yiorgos, a light snow was falling when the same two men in their little truck appeared on the road, carrying a brand new appliance box upright which, when we opened it, was an entirely different model. But then, we were so grateful to have refrigeration again, we decided not to mention it.

AND THE LIVIN' IS EASY

With the muses of Helicon let us begin our singing.

Hesiod

A month after Spiros planted the grapevines, I heard a distant sawing and hammering across the road on his property. Two men were building what would become a barn which would house and feed up to thirty sheep and goats. A month after the sheep and goats arrived, a horse appeared. And then a dozen chickens and a rooster. All were housed on the other side of the ridge so we never heard from them, but from time to time Spiros let me feed the animals. With adrenalin running through me, afraid they'd bite my hand off – God, I'd never been so close to so many large animals – I stuffed hay into a manger, while being pushed about by the herd of hungry beasts. Then into the coop, on whose low doorway I banged my head going both in and out, where I tossed feed to big cackling birds who could peck your eyes out. It was a thrilling addition to my new life, part of my own ongoing education. Spiros eventually planned to build a house on the land. He had already planted a large hillside garden where he would grow rows of perfect vegetables in the summer, which, besides family, he would distribute to his workers and friends including, happily, us.

By mid June, the first vegetables were ripe for picking: zucchini, eggplant, cucumber, romaine, and arugula. When he discovered I had bought the same kinds of vegetables from the markets he was upset, especially since his were all organic and some were even rotting while waiting to be picked. So part of my morning became walking through the rows of tomatoes on trellises, peppers, squash, melons, beans winding around poles, picking what we needed for the day, then banging my head going in and out of the small door to his hen house for eggs. I was enjoying all my daily chores immeasurably, going from one to another, while looking forward to the next, and in between riding my hog, my 100 CC motorbike, twenty-five miles an hour with a plastic produce basket fastened to the back, perfect for lugging around the day's groceries, the wind in my face, rolling along the main road by the sea on my way to the village, passing the large yachts at anchor, and sun bathers and swimmers enjoying the sun, men and women of all sizes, shapes and ages, in briefs and bikinis, their fleshy forms like desert landscapes.

Having taken a lesson from the old men on motorbikes, who had grown up on the backs of donkeys before there were roads and cars on the island, I insisted on taking my time, *siga siga*, no faster than if I were riding a bicycle pumping my brains out. Then, bouncing down the narrow cobblestone streets in the village, I would be off to the post office for the mail, where I would try to make Angeliki the postmistress smile shyly, or I would be weaving through the crowd on Papadiamanti Street to get the paper.

One of my first stops every morning was to Katerina's fruit and home grown vegetable market, because she had the largest variety on the island. It wasn't unusual to hear her husband yelling at her or their two sons through the old canvas, which hung low to block out the sun. The old man, with his scruffy white beard, usually sat smoking on an upside down plastic produce basket in jeans and layered wool, in the furthest corner from his wife, scheming, planning, glaring, scowling – an activity rarely seen in Skiathos. Sometimes, Katerina would yell back but she knew it was useless as she weighed my vegetables and gave me a look.

"When I married him he was a Greek God, now he's just a goddamn Greek." Poor sweet pudgy Katerina, a reminder that not all love stories have happy endings, with her sly sidelong glance, telling me as a joke she couldn't wait to die to get away from him. Surprising me with how quickly she was learning English, I looked forward to stopping there every day, even for an apple, just to teach her a new word and make her laugh. She loved to laugh, and I could make her hoot just by repeating with mock indignation the price she was asking for something in earshot of another customer. No one could explain why Katerina had become so addicted to this man. When she met him, he was married with two children and always seemed to be in a rage, and she was a head taller than him and nearly half his age. People even remember that she was rather attractive at the time and was concentrating on learning languages in a high school in Volos, run by French nuns. But Katerina was madly in love and he, bewitched, left his wife and children and she followed him to Skiathos and bore his children before he even got a divorce. Once on Skiathos, he used his only asset, a small truck, and brought vegetables from the mainland to markets in Skiathos. After a time, he had saved enough to open his own small produce stand on the road around the village, installing Katerina to run it. In a few years, he made a good bargain on a five hundred year old olive grove and uprooted all but a few of the trees to make room for a nursery and greenhouse where he grew anything that was possible to sell in his stand, which he constantly expanded and relocated to make room for groceries.

The eldest boy, Angelos, the larger and more rugged of the two brothers, was a good natured man in his early thirties who worked tirelessly, always looking down as if expecting a whack from a stick at any moment. The younger son, Nikos, taller, thinner, more delicate, was always the smartest in his class, until the day he was a senior in high school and his father told him he couldn't go to college and become an engineer, but had to stay home and work alongside his older brother. Now in his late twenties, humorless and sadly bitter, he appeared broken in spirit with the permanent scowl of his father. Despite the family dysfunction, Katerina and her boys seemed to like each other and would even smile from time to time in a conspiratorial aside to one another. But the three were continually on tiptoes, especially the brothers who, although towering over their father, sheepishly obeyed or avoided him altogether, working like serfs for their master, a life devoid of the company of anyone outside the family, let alone the occasional date or slightest hint of social life appropriate for single young men.

But it was Katerina who worked hardest of all, like a penance, paying for her sin. In addition to cooking the meals and washing the clothes and keeping house, seven days a week, fifty-two weeks a year, Christmas Day, Independence Day, when nobody on the island was working, Katerina, who had been growing ever larger over the years and with fewer teeth, would be standing behind a counter just large enough for a scale and a cash box from eight in the morning until eight at night. Covered only by a canvas roof, in the winter she would be bundled in heavy clothes with mittens, a knit cap pulled over her ears, and scarf covering her mouth and cheeks, standing hugging herself, shifting from foot to foot trying to keep warm, or making lunch on a hotplate in the back for the family who would eat standing, always on the run.

The English called her Mrs. Socks because she always wore socks, winter and summer. Perhaps it was simply the need to ease the difficulty of standing fourteen hours a day, but even on the hottest day of a hot summer, when everyone was in a bathing suit and bare foot, Katerina wore socks and heavy shoes, a print dress and a baseball cap, the exception being the rare occasion when she had a perm and dye and discarded the cap, and everyone commented on how nice she looked, which always made her eyes sparkle and her chubby cheeks blush.

One day, it was clear she had been crying. When I asked her what was wrong, she nodded over to her husband sitting in the corner, blistering mad. I jokingly told her she ought to take him out back and shoot him. She looked at me curiously. I leaned in close to her and made a gun with my thumb and forefinger.

"Shoot him. Bang bang. Who on the island would convict you?"

Her eyes widened. She looked at him and I could see she was imagining it. Then she looked back at me and howled and roared and called the boys over to tell them in Greek, and then she made a gun with her hand and fired off a couple in his direction and they all laughed and for the next few days, when I would ask her how her day was going, she answered me by making a gun and firing off a few in his direction. Each time I would think to myself one day I might possibly witness what I had sown. I had become a part of Katerina's life and she was a part of mine, like Yiorgos our stationer, his brother Nikos our pharmacist, Angeliki the postmistress, and many others on the island whose new faces had become like old friends. Having torn ourselves away from our old life, the reweaving of the new was now complete and all that was left was to live it.

By late June, the sea had become warm enough for me to grit my teeth and jump in, and since the water became measurably warmer each day, I was encouraged to immerse myself sooner the next time. By the first of July, I was wearing a bathing suit on my way to the village and, on my way home, I would simply pull my motorbike over almost anywhere and jump into the sea, and by the time I walked into the house, between the sun and the wind, my suit would be dry.

Even though I had been retired for a year and a half and my

life had become a vacation, I was feeling as if I was now on a real vacation and I had the summer off, just like when I was in grade school in Vermont and could spend the day mindlessly splashing in a pond. Anthea spent many hours happily in bed, reading books and doing puzzles. It was a glorious time.

In mid July, it suddenly turned unseasonably hot and humid for a week and we lunched in different tavernas at different beaches, first ordering an octopus salad or an omelet, or cheese pie and wine, then taking a swim while our order was being filled. The water was even more refreshing than the first sip of an ice cold beer. Since the Mediterranean is a body of water whose only access to the ocean is an eight mile strait between Spain and Africa, it has almost no tides or currents. Since it has a high salt content, on a windless day you can actually lie on your back and fall asleep in the water, waiting for your lunch to arrive, unable to keep a slow small smile from freezing on your face.

At some point, during the late spring, an eerily yellow-eyed pure black tom started coming around the kitchen door insinuating himself, making meowing demands. I had never been around cats except for the day when I was four and watched in horror as my oldest brother and a cousin set one on fire and dropped him from the attic window. Whether from guilt or indifference, I never sparked to cats. And I wasn't fooled by this one, trying to appear as cute and cuddly and tame as possible. I suspected it was only an act and I imagined if he were much larger, he'd be looking at me the way I'd seen him look at a cicada while playing with it, until he had slowly tortured it to death, crunched it between his teeth and spit it out.

Anthea originally called him Epaminondas, after a famous Greek general, but it became too hard to say. Like her grandfather, *pappou* in Greek, the tom liked to scratch his back against a wall, so Epaminondas became Pappou. The tom could care less. He was too busy trying to get a free meal while trying to placate his mistress who, we weren't aware, was pregnant at the time with a litter only a few weeks away. Skiathans love their cats, which are everywhere. The island is populated with strays that hang around tavernas in the summer and garbage cans in the winter, and eat scorpions and snakes and are generally welcomed, picked up and petted by anyone within arm's reach.

I thought I had seen Pappou at a distance a number of times when I was with Guido who, as a result of years of torture by neighboring cats, had become a notorious cat killer. After Guido died, the tom ventured closer and closer until, one day, there he was at Anthea's feet, rolling over and rubbing up against her, and Anthea was now finding little things for him to eat.

My neighbor told me he thought he'd seen the cat near a *kalivi* up the road, but he didn't think he actually belonged to anybody. And Anthea was now putting cat food on the shopping list and Pappou was coming around in the morning and evening, and Anthea would become concerned if he missed a meal, and now tic and flea spray were on the shopping list. And then unexpectedly, a fat grey and white cat started coming around with the tom, and I would shoo her away because of the horror of not being able to say "no" like Peter and Sharon, an expatriate couple on the island, who arrived with four cats and now had approximately twenty-six, which was only the group they allowed indoors. As Aeschylus wisely noted, "It is in the character of very few to honor without envy a friend who has prospered." For days I watched a dispute erupt between Pappou and his girl. He was getting fed and she wasn't. Somehow it was Pappou's fault. He shouldn't be going there if she couldn't eat there as well. For the first few days the fight was verbal, hissing and meowing, then the battle got physical. Several times I was awakened by a cat fight and Pappou would show up for his meal with pieces of fur missing and, while he meekly went into the house to eat, his girl would watch scowling from the hillside.

A few weeks later, I stepped out onto the patio and almost stepped on one of six or seven kittens, ranging from Pappou black to mama's grey and white. Having never been around cats, I reacted rather hysterically, dancing and twisting and clapping and screaming, then racing for the hose and chasing the herd up through the hillside with a stream of water that I was hoping would send a strong signal to this group that they were not welcome. I felt guilty on the one hand but, on the other, I felt we could easily become Peter and Sharon. A few days went by before I looked out my window in the morning and saw four kittens looking down at the terrace from the hillside. I raced downstairs and out of the house in a flash and sprayed the brats with the hose as they scampered away. It was several days later when a single kitten, similar in color to his mother, came back and boldly planted himself on the terrace. I sprayed him but, when I put the hose down, he came back and sat on the terrace defiantly. Again I sprayed and again he came back. For three days it continued. I admired his spunk. Finally, in a change of tactic, I ignored him and, after a few days, I realized one morning he hadn't been around. I suddenly missed him, but I never saw him again.

Pappou's girlfriend still came around occasionally. He still tried to woo and seduce her, play with her, and she would allow herself to be seduced and be playful but, if she moved too close to the kitchen door, he would kill her. And she tried. And he tried. Most days, Pappou hung around just outside that kitchen door, for although he had a little house that Anthea had arranged by the barbeque in case of rain, he was still an outdoor cat. Sometimes, he'd be gone for days and Anthea would worry he'd been killed by some Guido somewhere or murdered by Maria who was afraid of all cats, because as a child one jumped on her back and she couldn't shake it off. But before too many meals had been missed, Pappou would be back, rolling over, scratching his back against your shins. Maria said he was getting so fat we should enter him in the Guinness Book of World Records for his head alone. I actually fed him one day. It felt good. In sharp contrast to the lumbering goats and flailing chickens, Pappou was soft and gentle, but his tongue was like sandpaper.

As I began to know him better, I felt myself being drawn back into having the joy of a pet, something I had resisted after burying Guido. Clearly, it was time for Anthea and me to talk again about a pet, although probably still too soon to actually get one. For now, just talking about one would be enough.

Living away from close friends and family made the time you actually did get to spend together precious and coveted. Only the closest made the trip to Skiathos over the summer months, staying an average of two weeks. Travelling the long distance from America to Europe, then a plane change to Athens, then a boat or another plane, layovers, delays, was too difficult for our "I'll-call-you,-we'll-have-lunch" friends. In April, Goldie Hawn had e-mailed that she would be in Amsterdam in July on a book tour and would be free for nine days, and she and Kurt Russell were thinking of visiting us. We would recreate the time we spent together on Anthea's and my honeymoon in Tuscany. Anthea had known Goldie from the time she designed her costumes for the movie Shampoo, and they had been friends ever since and even partners in a movie company for a time, producing nine movies together. Now, Goldie was on a tour promoting her autobiography nonstop for weeks and was exhausted, and Greece was exactly what she needed.

Goldie and Kurt originally met on a movie for Disney in which Kurt, a child star, was playing a sixteen year old in The One and Only Genuine Original Family Band and Goldie, her first part in a movie, played a giggly girl. Years later, when Anthea and Goldie were meeting leading men for their movie

Swing Shift, a World War II story about a woman first tasting independence, Kurt would walk in following Kevin Costner and, true to the script where their characters would work together and fall in love in spite of themselves, Goldie and Kurt began playing together and fell in love in spite of themselves, and after twenty-five years were still in love and playing together, and now she and Kurt were coming to Skiathos to recapture what Kurt had recently told me was the best vacation he had ever had.

Skiathos was a small island which had a number of very important and successful people who had homes here or visited or had visited. One wealthy ship owner confided to me he once had a visit from Teddy Kennedy. But movie stars were different. The dream machine created gods, of which the Greeks were particularly fond. So it was of no small moment when I walked into Stagopolos' Hertz office and requested to reserve a jeep for Goldie and Kurt. Stagopolos screamed, stood from his desk, grabbed his head and twirled.

"I'm going to be renting one of my cars to Goldie Hawn and Kurt Russell! I don't believe it!"

It was Kurt who first raced into the baggage claim area grinning and skidded to a stop in sandals, typical Greek light white cotton pants and shirt, and a colorful Greek sash he once bought on the island of Santorini.

"Don't I look Greek?"

When Kurt walks into a room the light brightens, quite literally, inexplicably. Hugs with quiet laughter, pure joy, and then Goldie appeared, dragging her feet until she saw Anthea and broke into a huge smile.

They were excited to see our new house and had suggestions for further improvements like more terraces and landscaping, an infinity pool, guest *kalivis*, vineyards, embellishments one might make when the next few ships came in. Dreamers all, we listened and discussed, walked and measured, taking the greatest pleasure in old friends, spending what is more valuable than anything else, time. Kurt was especially taken by the aspect of the house. It was a superbly clear day and he was dazzled by the green of the island against the Mediterranean blue sea and the purple mountains in the background and, like me wherever I roamed, he was already talking about looking at property.

Running late for dinner, we piled into our jeep and rushed into the village to a taverna called Amfiliki, situated on a cliff overlooking the sea, where the food, which was prepared by Christos' mother, wife, and sister, was some of the best on the island. I suggested as one appetizer something I always ordered, Shrimps and Mushrooms Méditerranée, which was simply shrimp and mushrooms sautéed in oil with a squeeze of lemon and a drop of ouzo, and which Goldie liked so much she ordered again and, when she woke up the next morning, she said she dreamt about it and insisted we go back again that night. Which we did. And when she was eating a double order, this time for her entrée, she announced:

"This is the best food I've ever had anywhere in the world! Ever!" I couldn't disagree.

Driving away from the restaurant in the rain, trying to navigate a sharp turn on a very narrow street, I happened to run over a large snake that had wandered too close to the village and had been lying dead in the road before I realized it was there. The car thumped over it.

"What was that?"

"A branch in the road" I lied. To make matters worse I had to back over it to make the corner. Scrunch.

"It's a snake!" Kurt spotted it.

"Is it? Well, it was already dead."

"Yuck!"

"Oh, poor snake!"

Scrunch again trying to make the corner, and when I

couldn't, Kurt started to laugh, whereupon Goldie and Anthea scolded him until we had scrunched back over it again, then howls from everyone just before we had to roll over him one final time in order to be on our way.

Goldie went to bed first, then Anthea a few hours later, while Kurt and I sat on the terrace and drank wine and argued American politics until first light. Goldie never actually fell asleep and occasionally would rail at Kurt's libertarian views from her bed next to the open window above.

Early that morning, our phone started ringing:

"Can we send someone from the mayor's office to offer his compliments?"

Tasoula called, "Would Goldie and Kurt like a little publicity? I'm getting calls from Thessalonika!"

An Englishwoman we hardly knew, "Can I bring my daughter up to meet Goldie?"

Baskets of flowers, wine and cheese, fruits fresh and dried, sweets of all kinds arriving, some even for Anthea and me from the mayor with a note on his official paper:

"We are honored to have you living with us on our island."

Our stock was rising.

It rained off and on for the next few days. Goldie slept late, exhausted. Kurt was up and dressed and sitting at the dining table at seven every morning studying maps, first of Skiathos, then the Sporades, then calculating flying time in a Piagio airplane he was dreaming about buying, from Skiathos airport to thirty or forty capitals throughout Europe, Africa, and Asia:

"Istanbul, two hours. Cairo, three and a quarter."

After a coffee, he'd take an hour's walk around the mountain roads, then we'd go to town where I would do my morning chores. Kurt would happily tag along, curious about everything, excited about what I now perceived as ordinary narrow cobble stoned streets, small white Greek houses with brightly painted shutters, the simplicity of the village, the baker, the

small butcher shop. It was fun to see life on a small Greek island through his eyes.

For the first few days, when we returned from the village,
Goldie would be standing at the dining room glass door in a
white nightie, looking out over the valley at the rain, sipping
tea from a mug, a sweet smile when she saw Kurt.

By now we had a routine when guests came. The first night,
Amfiliki, the first lunch, Nostos Beach Taverna for an omelet
and some wine on the beach and a little swim, and so forth
for a whole perfect week which culminated, but only if you
wished, in a sail around the island on a tour boat which turned
in towards the shore at Banana Beach, a well-known nude
beach, where the boat slowed and hooted its horn, and then
was subsequently mooned by all the days' sun worshippers as
it chugged out of the bay. Little kids especially loved that part
of the tour.

How quickly guests seemed to prefer this taverna or that
beach and wanted to return over and over, perhaps helping
them feel less adrift. It seemed that people needed anchors,
even on vacation. Goldie and Kurt had no such need. Other
than the Shrimps Méditerranée, Goldie and Kurt wanted to see
everything, do everything, eat everything, and in the back of
their minds there was beginning to form the following thought:

"Wouldn't it be great to have a house here?"

And Kurt would measure, "Only five hours to Kenya" "Less
than four hours to London."

Within three days, they wanted to look at land for sale. Kurt
on one of his walks had already picked out a spread which he
thought had a fabulous view and land enough for several guest
houses, a pool, a vineyard, and so on, but was it one parcel, was
it for sale, and was there something better around?

Enter Geof. Goldie, Kurt, Anthea and I followed him in
his dented pickup to a four-acre property on a bluff overlooking the sea, with a breathtaking mountain landscape and sea

views to Euboea and the mainland. Goldie and Kurt became excited.

"This is where the main house would be!"

"I think the vineyard should be over there!"

"What is the cost per square foot to build here?"

In the distance, we began to hear the faint yet ever stronger sound of disco music from down below as we continued to walk the land.

"We could build a barn for a few horses! It's a great place to ride!"

"A nice caretaker's cottage over there!"

The music became ever louder as a tour boat came into view with the thump thump thump of disco music blaring, forcing us to shout to be heard.

For the rest of their stay they would venture out alone for part of every day and drive and walk together all over the island, continuing to look at property, walking beaches, enjoying quiet time together. People were getting used to them being around and, although they never went unnoticed, for the most part they were left alone.

The following weekend Robert and Hope arrived. Robert had in fact been with Goldie and Kurt and us in Italy and so it was even more of a reunion. Watching him now with Kurt, giving as good as he got, but always respectful, I was reminded of how much he had developed in the few years from the boy in Italy to the man today. And I realized that not only did the expanse between us help him spread his wings but, when we did come together, it allowed me to view him as if for the first time.

To mark the occasion I decided we should roast a whole lamb in the traditional Greek style in our barbeque, although we didn't have the faintest idea how. I invited Spiros and his family and told him my lamb plan and asked for guidance.

"One of mine" Spiros insisted. "A baby. I ask Takis to come. He's the best for roasting lamb. No stress, we do everything."

On Sunday, Spiros and his cousin Takis, a strong, handsome, grey haired man in his fifties, arrived at eleven in the morning with Spiros' lamb, slaughtered and skinned earlier in the week and hung to drain for five days, now wrapped in garbage bags. Takis, if you were to give him an Italian gangster's nickname, would be "No Nonsense." He was the master. In life he was the first engineer ever on the island but now, with the ease of a man whose job in life might have been to make a large barbeque fire, he made piles of coals over the entire bed of the barbeque and started them with pinecones and twigs he quickly gathered from the immediate area, explaining to me while he was fanning the piles with his hand that they were to allow air to pass between them to let the fire breathe. Then, Takis and Spiros pushed the large skewer through the lamb and, using pliers and two kinds of wire, they secured the lamb to the skewer so quickly and skillfully that I realized I would have to watch them more than a few times to be anything more than a man dressed as a lamb roaster. Every so often Takis would put his hand a foot above the coals and depending on how long he could keep it there would be the indicator for when the fire was ready. Finally, the lamb was roasting, as it rotated with the help of an electric motor, and the three of us took turns basting it, constantly checking the temperature of the coals. For the next six hours, it was baste, check, baste, check. It might sound like work but we chit chatted and drank wine and the time went quickly as the lamb slowly turned brown.

In the meantime, Anthea, a triple Libra, the sign of order and design cubed, who planned a dinner the way a choreographer carefully planned a dance, had laid out the table in the dining room with a centerpiece of flowers and a buffet of salads and vegetables, breads and cheeses, then tastefully set out two tables on the terrace for sixteen people. Matoula and the family arrived with cheese pies and bitter greens, sweets and wine. Anthea meticulously rearranged everything on the dining room table together with plates, napkins, and silver.

Kurt and Robert were at the barbeque, passing out bites of the lamb that Takis was cutting off the rotating carcass, and I was racing around tending drinks when Takis suddenly announced the lamb was ready and it wouldn't wait one more minute, and the whole family was suddenly on their feet, and as Takis cut the lamb onto the platters, the family hurried into the dining room, took all the plates and silver, napkins, salads, breads, cheeses, cheese pies, vegetables and scattered them all over the tables on the terrace. "Good God", I thought, "Anthea!"

I raced into the kitchen and found exactly what I expected, Anthea, near tears, hugging herself, her table ruined, both tables ruined, all three tables ruined. I put my arms around her and reminded her of the vital lesson I learned in front of the bank.

"It's Greece, eh?"

Sighing, she wiped her eyes as she passed into the dining room, picked up the salt and pepper mills, then swept out onto the terrace with a smile and a look of self assurance as if the aforementioned chaos had all been part of her plan.

The lamb was indescribable, except to say I was not worthy and I suspect I'll never have the likes of it again. We ate and drank the perfect wine which Spiros had brought, then retired to the living room where I sat at the piano and played the two Greek songs by the hugely gifted songwriter Mikis Theodorakis. The Greeks all sang, Anthea the loudest. Afterwards, Goldie sang Summertime and even Kurt was singing during Amazing Grace and then Takis asked if I knew another particular song of Theodorakis, which I didn't, and which he started to hum. The others quickly joined in and clapped and Anthea started dancing, and Goldie danced and Kurt sat with what one might call a shit-eating-grin on his face, and it was a great summer night and there was a cool breeze from the north floating through the room, and I was especially happy because Robert was there, and I turned from the piano and clapped along with my own shit-eating grin from the joy of having so many people I loved in the same room at the same time. The day after Goldie and Kurt left, the mayor's office again called early in the morning:

"Someone told the mayor Mel Gibson is staying in your house!"

Two days later, they called again:

"Richard Gere?"

Anthea suggested the next time they call just say yes, but please don't tell anyone, then hang up and watch our stock soar.

For the next three weeks we had Robert and Hope to ourselves. Robert rented a motorbike and the two of us explored the back roads and small chapels dotting the island. At the Monastery, at Kechria, while drinking cool spring water with our hands, Robert said that the time we were spending together was indeed of a better quality than we would have had in the stress and strain of Hollywood. As we sat on a stone bench in silence for the next few minutes, looking out at the sea, father and son, I was mindful of the fact that for me these moments were the best of the best of times.

In late July, the air seemed suddenly cooler and it was becoming noticeably darker earlier. At the end of July, the Meltemi, a north wind, started every mid day, became strongest in the afternoon and ended in the early evening. It kept the island cool during the hottest time of year. In August, I soon learned not to try to get a part for a car or an appliance serviced. It was as if the companies never existed. All of Europe was on vacation. August 15th, the day celebrated as the Assumption of the Virgin Mary, was the summer's biggest and most important holiday throughout South Europe. Greek Public Radio was playing only Maria and Mary songs. The island was bursting at the seams with every room occupied, and people sleeping

on beaches and in parks and cars. At the port, there was a sar-
dine festival in the evening where they would be passing out
sardines with crusty bread and wine. There was dancing, but
Anthea and I stayed home and ate under the pergola, then shut
the lights and talked late into the night about her father and
other phantoms. Our friendship was also deepening, the sweetest part of growing old together.

All summer, along the road around Strofilia Pond, the small
hotels had been alive with guests. The pools and bars and tavernas were bulging with people. Mihalis's three tavernas were
consuming the tomatoes from those three thousand plants he'd
been cultivating. All his rooms were full and his many businesses flourishing, yet he preferred to stay in the smallest of the
three tavernas, his first one, greeting customers, waiting tables,
making sure the kitchen ran smoothly. This was also his season
to be working. Across the road were his goats grazing within
view, as if Mihalis set them there for ambiance. He always spotted me before I could see him as I walked by.

"I'm thinking about you!" Then, insisting I have a coffee or
a wine, "Water is for frogs! Have a piece of melon. From my
garden!"

Even during the hottest time of year Skiathos had remained
green: the pines, the olive trees, shrubbery and even much of
the field grass. My summer dance card had been almost too full.
Having had dinner in Hollywood once or twice a week with
close friends and family, when you barely scratched the surface
of each other before adjourning until the next time, when once
again you started scratching, was not the same as living under
the same roof for a few weeks as a family. It had been fun ex-
ploring different beaches during the day and heavenly sitting
out on our terrace at night, looking towards the sea under the
Milky Way, watching the moon traverse a starlit sky. The wine,
the quiet, the moonlight on the sea, the late night discussions

and confessions, all served to deepen the friendships. Everyone told us in their own way we were beyond lucky. They loved the island and all raved about the food. Even the most persnickety was easily satisfied.

As the season flew by, there were so many days and nights that I wished could have lasted forever and, on September 1st, when Maria brought one of the new crop of pomegranates to the house and rolled it onto the floor for good luck for the year, I needed a sweater to sit outside, a taste of the autumn which would soon be upon us. By the time the schools opened in the second week of September, as quickly as the island had swelled from six to sixty thousand, it was back to around six. All the hotels and tavernas were still open and the sea still warm, but the roads were empty again and it seemed as if the island was a playground exclusively for the few of us left behind. But we were both tired. The summer was intense and we were looking forward to the quiet of winter. We knew it would be long, and without a project like building a house, I wondered what would occupy us. I was eager to know the answer. But I would have to wait. And see.

SELEGOUDI

A very civilized people in a small place.

Grigoris Giannakouros

Sometime in the late summer, we were sitting in Volos, in Rodia, a taverna where they had already closed the doors at 2:00 a.m. but would be continuing to serve wine on the house, and where the three guitar players, three *bouzouki* players, two girl singers, a harmonica player, and a man on spoons would continue to sit around a large round table and play and sing folk songs of love, sorrow and hashish from the '20s. "From this small village thirty or forty became quite successful" smiled Grigoris Giannakouros, a stiff, stern, elegant man in his early seventies, Anthea's cousin, whom she was meeting for the first time. At seventeen, Grigoris Giannakouros left his tiny village of Selegoudi in the mountains below Sparta for college and became a high-ranking executive of the National Bank of Greece. Now retired and living in the Pelion mountains above Volos, Grigoris was an old family friend of our lawyer on Skiathos who, when she first heard Anthea's maiden name and father's birthplace, realized they were related and arranged to bring the two cousins together. The evening for me was a delightful distant blur of cigarette smoke, wine, and song, but it lit a flame in Anthea to once again see her father's village in the Peloponnese, so in early October we decided to take a drive.

I didn't have confidence in the jeep, so Stagopolos from Hertz lent us a car: *"Kalo taxidi!"*, good voyage, he bid us. And as we pulled away, "Please don't dent it!" Bruce and Marcia had a friend who organized and led motorcycle road trips through the Peloponnese to which Bruce, the history teacher, had contributed by plotting an itinerary of historical sites and cities. He insisted we take a copy and, if we followed it, we would have a great trip. Except for Volos, we hadn't been out of our sphere in over a year and, besides the sentimental journey for Anthea, we were looking forward to seeing more of Greece. The itinerary seemed wonderfully planned: lunches by the sea, dinner and lodging in the mountains, seeing the important historical and natural sites, walking in places I'd read about, Corinth, where we would have coffee overlooking the canal, Epidauros, an ancient health spa that, besides mineral waters and herbal baths and massages, had an outdoor theatre as part of the treatment, the ancients believing theatre provided a catharsis which played an important part in replenishing the health of the whole body. The theatre itself was a structure of stone blocks which seated 10,000, with acoustics so perfect you could crinkle a piece of paper at center stage and hear it clearly in the 85th row a hundred fifty feet above. When I finally stepped on the splendid stone stage, I immediately and inexplicably felt a powerful energy surge through me. It was astonishing. I had a burning impulse to do a monologue, act out one of the great speeches of one of the ancient Greek playwrights, a tragedy with a moral, a comedy with social significance. I was having an epiphany which illuminated the last thirty-five years, giving them a context I hadn't considered, that those years were worthwhile in a whole other way.

After an excellent lunch by the sea, we went to Mistras, a Byzantine walled city, then to the Diros caves where we were rowed around in a little fishing boat for a fascinating mile underground, then to Olympia, Mycenae, Ancient Nemea, each site with its own great history. Then, for an hour we would wind our way up a high mountain towards Sparta to Anthea's father's birthplace, Selegoudi, a hamlet without a gas station or store of any kind, a few acres of tableland with a few modest houses, a small church and school. It looked deserted when we pulled into the empty main square, which was also the church parking lot. She had only been there once as a child and it was not at all as she had remembered. It was confusing and spoiling her childhood memory and she didn't want to get out of the car. But I was curious that from these simple dwellings came so many successful men. I insisted we at least look around. Slowly, silently walking towards the row of five or six houses, looking for a sign of life, even a sound, until in the middle of the group in a small yard, we saw an old woman cutting roses. I tried to push Anthea towards her but she resisted, being too shy to speak, so I jumped in.

"*Kalimera.*"

The old woman had been following us out of the corner of her eye and wasn't startled by my voice. She looked over, curious, so I spoke Anthea's surname.

"Giannakouros?"

The woman squinted at me and looked me up and down as if I were a member of the secret police and spoke a few words like, "Who wants to know?", at which time Anthea found her tongue. She stepped up and said she was Anthoula Giannakouros and her father was so and so and were there any relatives around. The old woman's eyes widened and she slipped her shears into her apron, then wiped her hands on the hem and opened the little gate. Looking up at Anthea for a moment, she grinned wide, and tearfully hugged her:

"You look just like your grandmother Anthoula."

Within five minutes there were two long tables set up on her porch with lace cloths. Cousins began appearing from everywhere, a woman walking down the path carrying a colander

filled with potatoes, a man from the little house next door carrying a large jug of wine on his shoulder, another with a basket
of bread, a woman with a plate of vegetables and, within thirty
minutes, Anthea and I and twenty relatives were sitting eating cold meat, grilled meat and vegetables, salads, cold pastas,
cheeses, cheese pies, breads, fruit, olives, wine, cakes and talking about Anthea's paternal grandmother, her namesake. Although it was a working class family, everyone dressed in their
best casual clothes for the event, men in gabardine trousers and
perfectly ironed starched shirts, women in skirts and blouses or
dresses. Even the old woman had quickly shed her apron and
changed into a grey print dress. I was touched that they would
put on their good clothes for us, who were wearing jeans, and I
wondered how far down the mountain it was to a dry cleaner.

As they shared stories with Anthea in Greek, and because
the language was gibberish to me, I was free to study them,
their faces and bodies, and behavior. And as I watched Anthea,
her eyes wet from recalling her grandmother, I could see her in
them and them in her, and how deeply roots were responsible
for who you were. Besides seeing her nose on this man and her
mouth on that woman, it helped explain so much about her,
her love of and important regard for food, for the importance
of leftovers, the timbre of her voice, the depth of her laugh, the
ability to be utterly familiar with others she barely knew, to
respond without editing, to be thoughtful, philosophical.

No one actually lived in Selegoudi anymore. Like many of
the smaller remote mountain villages in Greece, the people had
moved to the cities for jobs: Sparta, Athens, and Thessalonika.
But many kept up their homes and land in their old villages
and returned every year during different parts of the summer
and fall, ever attached to their land, their village, and to each
other. For the old people, it provided continuity in their lives,
a starting and ending point, both of which would be in that
hamlet. For the younger, it would probably eventually only be

the family cemetery, but now it was the place they all felt most comfortable, most familiar. We were lucky to catch them before they left for the winter. Having harvested their olives and made their wine, this would be their last weekend until next spring.

Anthea's grandfather, Thomas Giannakouros, son of the owner of the olive press in the village, became self-educated by reading the ancients and insisted his four sons do the same. Discovering classical music in the United States where he worked as a chef, he brought back a gramophone and classical records to broaden his sons' horizons. His dream was to give them a formal education so, unlike him, they might become professionals. One son would later become a Supreme Court Judge in Greece; one would become head of the legal department for Shell Oil in Greece, and one a very influential lawyer in Athens, who would marry the daughter of the Minister of Finance. Anthea's father, the eldest, met and married her mother while on vacation in New York, and subsequently stayed in America and became successful enough that he would think nothing of picking up the night's tab for sixteen people at the Copacabana once or twice a week.

But it was only after three hours of eating and drinking that Anthea realized we were sitting with only relatives of Anthoula's Maravelias family. There was not a single Giannakouros at the table. In the next hour, Anthea asked if her grandfather Thomas Giannakouros' house was still standing. It was a ruin, she was told, and her uncles had plenty of money to have kept it in good condition, but they all became big shots in Athens and decided they were too good to have anything to do with the village. It was precisely at that point Anthea nudged me it was time to take our leave. One of the older men said he'd show us Thomas' house. Even with a sore arm I could have thrown a stone and hit it. Thirty yards away, hidden at the end of a driveway below the road was the deserted ruin, while next to it stood an elegant stone house where a middle aged man and an old woman were sitting on the terrace sipping coffee.

"Giannakouros", the old man confided with a sneer, then shook our hands as he bid us goodbye, "Anthoula, you know your father still has olive trees in Selegoudi!" Then, he threw the Giannakouros a cool glance, turned and walked quickly back up the driveway.

Uninvited to the wonderful lunch was an elegant and handsome woman in her late seventies, first cousin to Anthea's father, and her architect son, both fashionably and expensively dressed, who insisted we join them. As the three of them became acquainted, the woman sat erect and spoke carefully and precisely of the time the King and Queen stopped at her grandfather's house for coffee, and it dawned on me that one of the things I admired about Anthea was how easily she moved between groups of people and without exception treated them all the same. Whether as a coveted collaborator by notoriously difficult and highly intelligent Hollywood writers and directors, or as one who took great pleasure in playing cards and hanging out with the drivers or grips on a movie set, Anthea was equally at ease with both and without the slightest personality adjustment.

Because she had a very small family in New York which was mostly gone, and I had so little experience with them, our afternoon in Selegoudi allowed me the rare opportunity to place her in a context and, like a child's face which resembles each parent at different angles, I could see clearly for the first time where it was possible for her to be at once warm and fun loving like the Maravelias and also the witty, elegant Giannakouros.

On the drive home, after thinking it all over, I came to the conclusion that after knowing Anthea far better than any other human being, even to being able to finish many of her sentences, after thirty years together, I was still only scratching her surface. I suspected she had been feeling the same way about herself, though she never mentioned it. But I could tell by the reverence in which she now held Selegoudi that it had somehow become for her a starting point in defining herself. Away from the need to achieve and the fear of failure that she held since she could remember, Anthea was beginning to see herself in a whole other way. These were her people. What's more, she liked them. Enjoyed them. Felt at home among them. Both sides.

At the Maravelias' table, one old man was telling Anthea that her father used to send the village a box of his old clothes every year. Anthea was suddenly deeply touched as she turned and spoke softly to me:

"He once owned one of my father's suits."

GETTING INVOLVED

Democracy…a charming form of government
full of piety and disorder,
and dispensing a sort of equality to equals
and unequals alike.

Plato

The current mayor had been serving as the vice mayor when the previous mayor was indicted on corruption charges. I had been having a problem with the public road leading to my driveway, a hundred yards of which would become a mud mousse whenever it rained for two days in a row. The cement trucks would get stuck and we'd have to hire a tractor to free them, and the mayor was the one person on Skiathos who could order it to be graded and paved. My neighbors all told me the road was much, much better now. As children they remembered seeing donkeys stuck fast in mud up to their waist. Nevertheless, we couldn't wait for nature, so Spiros, who was in the same class in school with the mayor, said he would speak to him. Which he did, after which the mayor said he would look into it. Nothing. Then Loula's brother, Thomas, one of the elders and most highly respected men on the island, arranged an interview for me in the mayor's office during which he pleaded my case:

"The road is so bad he can't have important people like Goldie Hawn come to visit in the winter! It's not good for the island!"

The mayor nodded and said Thomas was right. He had acknowledged the importance of having guests like Goldie and
Kurt on the island as well as residents like Anthea and me, and
reminded Thomas that he had sent us gift baskets from the
municipality, and in fact had already sent someone to look at
the road and they had determined how to address the problem.
A month went by. Two months. Three. Nothing. Every time I
saw the mayor, he pretended he understood less English than
the last time I had spoken with him and, since I spoke no
Greek, he managed to slip through without properly account-
ing for his inability to act. The road was an important issue to
us, so I never ceased seeking him out and shaking his hand and
telling him he was doing a great job but our road was badly in
need of attention. One day, after I told him what a wonderful
idea it was to build a station house for people waiting for the
hydrofoil, he looked at me and said in broken English:

"The council voted to fix your road."

Then he smiled at me and I knew he was lying.

"*Efharisto*", I muttered. "*Efharisto para poli*." (Thank you
very much.) I shook his hand and backed away, feeling like
a bug that had just been brushed away from his lapel. Spiros
called him again. He told Spiros the road was in the pipeline
and that he would like to arrange to have dinner with us and
our wives, but he was too busy at the moment because he was
preparing to run for mayor in the coming election. When he
first took over the mayor's mantle, he did so only reluctantly.
A third generation fisherman, he was brought to the original
mayor's slate to attract those voters. But after a year of being
mayor, he had become fully aware of the power entrusted to
the office, and whatever dreams he might have had for the
island could to a large extent be realized if he exerted enough
energy and husbanded their resources. And it excited and
challenged him, and he had now become fierce about being
elected.

Although four candidates were running, the contest was essentially between the old mayor, a three term incumbent who had been severely scolded but not convicted for doling out free licenses for beach concessions to friends and family, depriving his partner, the central government of Greece, her due. In addition to being the only pediatrician and, if you had children, someone whose favor could even be critical, the old mayor also came from a large family and, in the years he was in charge, had managed to minister to 45% of the population, knowing that 42% was all that was needed to retain the seat. His main opponent was the current mayor whose concern was for the working people on the island and their needs. Hardly a choice.

Starting in college, politics had been an important part of my life. The head of my philosophy department, a brilliant Jesuit named Father Henry Kenney, persuaded me to march for civil rights and my eyes were opened. In Hollywood, I gave slide shows to clubs and groups and anyone who would watch and listen, arguing against U.S. involvement in Vietnam. For two years, our guesthouse in Hollywood was Congresswoman Barbara Boxer's home in Los Angeles while she campaigned for the U.S. senate seat from California, which she won. Anthea was also active, being one of the ten founding members of the Hollywood Women's Political Committee, raising millions of dollars, not for personal gain, but for candidates who would agree to support an agenda they were interested in, which included women's rights, the environment, and AIDS. With the announcement of the mayoral race, Anthea and I decided to learn about the two candidates, our road notwithstanding. It was our island too, our neighborhood, and we had some ideas and thought we might be able to make a difference.

To be among the people who had conceived democracy and to witness an election on a small Greek island may be a once in a lifetime lesson in the democratic process. Each of the four candidates had a slate of delegates, every one selected to attract a certain constituency. The slate which accumulated the most votes determined who was mayor. The city council would consist of delegates from different parties according to their individual vote count, thus insuring every faction was represented proportionally. As the campaign began, the islanders began referring to the two main candidates as "the pediatrician" and "the fisherman's son". Geof's daughter, Zoe, was on the fisherman's son's slate, hoping she would attract the ex pats. Olympia, our family doctor, was on the pediatrician's slate while the old doctor from the health center was on the fisherman's. Everyone had close relatives and friends running on opposing tickets and in many cases loyalties were in conflict with ideals. As the election approached, it became increasingly heated. With two weeks to go, the polls favored the pediatrician with his usual 44% while the fisherman's son trailed with 33%.

Tasoula was for the pediatrician, whom she considered the lesser of two evils. Spiros and his family were for the fisherman's son, even though Loula's nephew, Yiannis, was running as one of the four mayoral candidates. Lines were drawn. Mihalis told me that many of the lines reached back to the Civil War, which occurred shortly after the Second World War. The fisherman's son represented the liberals. The pediatrician was a conservative. The Civil War was bitter and bloody in most of Greece, but perhaps because on a small island everyone was so interdependent, they couldn't afford to be at war with anyone or they risked losing some essential item or service. The violence on Skiathos was limited to several fistfights, except for one notable incident. The conservatives were badly beating a communist by the quay, when his sister jumped into the fray and pushed him into the sea. People watching said she saved his life. And now, scores of years later, the war was still being fought by some, but in the political arena.

"The old mayor never spent any of the money on Skiathos!

He used it all to travel around the world and stay in the best hotels!" Obviously a liberal.

"The new mayor's an idiot! He didn't even go to college!" Obviously a conservative.

"The old mayor's a crook! He gave all the city jobs to friends and relatives!"

"The new mayor's not refined enough to represent Skiathos in the wider world!"

Posters were suddenly on telephone poles, extolling the virtues of each smiling candidate. Storefronts suddenly became campaign headquarters. Rumors began flying. "He's going to be indicted again!"

"I hear no one ever stole as much as this one!"

Then the mud.

When the opposition referred to the current mayor, they referred to him by the name Karabelas, a Turkish word meaning "black trouble", which the Skiathans had nicknamed his father. This served to remind the voter he wasn't a real Skiathan, but the son and grandson of fishermen who immigrated to the island from a small coastal village in Asia Minor near Smyrna, and which also helped the pediatrician underscore the difference in their class and breeding.

Everyone became more entrenched. Their candidate was undoubtedly superior.

"He's an absolute moron! He can't even speak Greek!"

"Because he didn't go to college you think he's a moron! You're the moron! The man graduated from the National Merchant Marine Academy with high honors!"

In truth, the first year we were on Skiathos, while the pediatrician was in charge, nothing changed. No apparent public work had been done. With the advent of the new mayor, there was a sudden flurry of changes. The decaying quay was being tastefully resurfaced with good tiles. A green was introduced by the port and planted with olive and elm trees. Old roads were being repaired. The streets were cleaner. In short, the island was being looked after in a way that in retrospect had been largely absent the previous year. I believed in clean streets and thought most of the people on the island would as well. And even though he was almost laughingly behind in the polls, I bet Papa Yiorgos' son-in-law, Kostas, 50 euros the fisherman's son would win. Two weeks before the election, the mayor called Spiros about scheduling that promised dinner. A few days later at our house, together with Spiros and Matoula, like political advisors, we gave the candidate the litany of complaints we had been hearing about him and his administration and what his best defense might be, never once mentioning the road. He listened, nodded, smiled, and I was feeling a little like that bug again. But we plodded on. We told him his winning had become important to us. We offered to host an evening for him at our house to meet, speak and listen to the expatriates who were registered voters. We would serve wine and hors d' oeuvres, which he thought was an excellent idea and decided to enlist Zoe to help us. Zoe and her husband thought it was such a good idea they decided to do it at their taverna on Papadiamanti Street, have an open bar, mezethes, and invite the whole town. Which they did. It was very well attended, especially when it was known the bar was completely open and the mezethes were excellent. The mayor spoke passionately about fixing potholes so your "*yiayia*", grandmother, wouldn't trip and break her hip when she went to IKA [Social Security Institute] and so you wouldn't get killed on your motorbike. The response was resounding and there was so much energy among the people, we began to think this underdog could possibly win.

It had been the custom on the island that each candidate gives a speech at a common public area on the Friday night before the Sunday election, each to be scheduled at different times so that the islanders could attend all of them. It was also the custom that the incumbent mayor be allowed to give the last of the speeches. This year, however, when the mayor posted his time on Friday night, the pediatrician posted the same time. And so, at two different public squares, no more than a hundred yards apart, two stages, two sets of gigantic speakers, and two crowds assembled, some even walking back and forth to try and hear the message of the other.

The balding pediatrician wore a warm and gentlemanly brown herringbone sport coat and brown slacks with a button down white shirt and red tie. The fisherman's son with his thick shock of jet black hair wore a thin worn black suit, possibly a half size too small. The pediatrician spoke in a honeyed soothing voice, telling his supporters what he would be doing beginning Monday morning, the many advantages businesses would have, the innovations for attracting more and better tourists. The fisherman's son railed and ranted about how the island had been neglected under the old mayor and pointed to all the improvements he was able to accomplish in such a short time and what he would continue to do, little things like a small shelter from the elements for school children while they waited for the school bus, and bigger things like turning the old garbage dump into a park. He spoke from the heart and with a great deal of power and passion and humor. The pediatrician spoke with reason, reassurance and humor. He would roll back the added service charge the fisherman's son had instituted for taverna owners who had outdoor café sections on the quay, which was city property.

On election Sunday, while Anthea was voting, an older man with deep creases in a strong, square face stepped over to me extending his hand:

"I'm Nikos. I own the land next to Thalia. Two over from you. Where is a driveway?"

I gripped his hand, "Oh, yes! Yes! Two over. That's your land, Nikos?"

"Yes. From my grandfather. You know, they start our road next week? Finally! It's on the schedule." He threw up his arms in mock disbelief, "The council vote it months ago!"

That night we watched the election results at Loula's house in the village, fifty yards from the current mayor's campaign headquarters. Skiathos, having its own television studio and radio station, started publicly announcing results as soon as the polls closed. With the first announcement came cheers and air horns from the mayor's headquarters. In the first of the eight precincts he was beating the pediatrician 52 to 34%. A major upset. As the evening went on, there were more and more shouts and air horns, then fireworks and finally church bells, as someone from the fisherman's son's party had climbed to the bell tower of the church and was ringing the bells. The fisherman's son had won an overwhelming victory, a clear clean sweep. Evidently, the people were more interested in sheltering their young children from the rain than lowering fees for taverna owners on the quay.

"The moron won! The island's going to hell!"

"A great victory for the people!"

Suddenly there was the sound of a *bouzouki* and several guitars from players who were standing in front of the fisherman's son's campaign office, and Thanassis, who owned the gym, was singing soulfully into a microphone and the streets were filling with supporters being led by the newly elected mayor in a block long sirto [traditional Greek line dance], down Papadiamanti Street, while the old white-haired Doctor from the health center, with a lit cigarette between his teeth and a spring in his step that would shame most young men, led another line going the opposite way. Anthea danced in the Doctor's line while I stood by and watched. Yiannis' father came over to thank me for our support, as did several others on the mayor's slate. It was a feeling I hadn't realized I had missed until now: that I had somehow made a difference.

In the morning, the election would be ancient history. The fight was over. The mud would be washed away. This was Greece and things were now settled by the ballot. Later in the month, all the wounds would be healed and the Greeks from all over the country would be brought together again as one nation in the form of a special national holiday.

After all, it was only politics.

OHI DAY

We knew thee of old, oh divinely restored
By the lights of thine eyes and the light of thy sword.
From the bones of our slain shall thy vigor prevail
And we greet thee again, hail liberty hail!

Greek National Anthem
Translated into English (1918) by Rudyard Kipling

Standing in our kitchen, drinking morning coffee less than two weeks after the election, I was watching the ferry from Volos creep along in the distant sea, listening to Greek National Public Radio where a woman was singing and Anthea was translating a popular love song from the Second World War, a time when 50,000 Athenians died of starvation.

"Please, don't send me flowers, send me a bag of zucchini."

It was already the 28th of October, the anniversary of the day in 1940, when Italy's dictator, Mussolini, demanded free passage through Greece and the control of strategic areas in the country. Knowing full well they were outgunned and outmanned and what it would mean, Ioannis Metaxas, the Greek dictator, reflecting the will of the people, said "OHI", NO, to Mussolini, a moment which forever after would define the Greeks as a nation. Finally free from the yoke of the Ottomans, even though small in numbers, the people would stand together and not allow themselves to be occupied ever again, and the war with Italy began. The Greeks fiercely fought the Italians back beyond the Albanian border, but the Germans invaded from Bulgaria and Yugoslavia and Athens was taken on the 27th of April 1941. To remind themselves and teach the younger generation of their elders' courage in the face of the starvation that followed, to define for themselves their national character, and to articulate the compact all Greeks had with each other regarding their liberty, an important national day of remembrance was established on the anniversary of that decision, "Ohi Day". At 10:30 in the morning, all the leaders in villages and cities throughout the nation would march in a procession to their war memorial where there would be a laying of wreaths.

By that time in October, Skiathans had closed and shuttered their seasonal shops and tavernas and were busy making their wine, picking, pressing and curing their olives. School had been in session over a month, the tourists and summer people had all left the island weeks ago. More donkeys were on the roads with men in wool riding sidesaddle, sheep were being herded on the ring road around the village, ewes had gone to the ram and with any luck, in five months the lambs would be born for Easter. For a few weeks there was an Indian summer and the roses burst into one final bloom before they slowly shut down. Hunting season had begun, hares, pheasants, partridge, fishing season had opened for trawlers, nuts were harvested, almonds, walnuts, pine nuts, and everyone was bringing us aubergines and quince from their gardens.

Although it was the middle of the week, every office and shop was closed, but there was a crackling energy in the morning air as Anthea and I strolled down Papadiamanti Street, the warm sun shining through a wispy thin layer of clouds, passing Skiathans in suits and Sunday dresses. It was interesting to see who was married to whom, two people you knew from different compartments in your life, coupled, their kids strolling alongside or playing quietly about in their school uniforms, navy and white, each grade having their own stamp, a different colored scarf or sweater. Others dressed in traditional Greek costumes with colorful embroidery, which originated in the mountain villages in the early 19th century and continued in much of rural Greece until the 1960s, and which still existed in one or two villages where they were not yet considered a costume, but clothing.

As we reached the port, the thirty-two piece Skiathos Philharmonic Band was gathering, so we stopped to say the usual holiday greeting in Greece *"Chronia pola"*, may you live many years, to Nikos, son of our florist, a very sweet and delicate young man who that day looked strangely small holding a big trombone in his maroon and navy military band uniform with its gold braid swag and his small navy peaked cap. The quay was lined with flags and the tavernas were already mostly full, but we found a ringside table and four chairs at Dimitra's taverna right next to the parade route, a narrow single lane of stones along the port, which in total ran about seventy-five yards. A police officer strolled by chuckling into a cell phone. Geof joined us wiped out from a five-day holiday in Istanbul where one of his travelling companions had her purse stolen. The sun was warming, so I took off my sweater. The breeze from the sea was cooling. Papa Nikolas, Papa Yiorgos' son, walked by surrounded by a gaggle of admiring young people, then Tasoula and Stamatis, Mercini with Danae, and Mitzos, our house painter, currently in love, looking remarkably invigorated. Almost everyone on the island had arrived on the quay by now. Suddenly, the band began playing and people lined the road. The young band leader counted off and began marching the band, which played the national anthem. The parade included a six-man palace guard in period costume, followed by a contingent which included the mayor, the Chief of Police of Skiathos, the Chief of the Port Police, the Chief of the Skiathos Fire Department, three priests and a monk, then the school children in their uniforms and costumes by grade, youngest first, the future of Skiathos, of Greece. I was touched. Innocent, proud, serious faces filled with hope, the high school gym teacher marching stiffly alongside the senior boys, blowing his whistle in cadence, then barking, *"Ena thio, ena thio"*, one two one two, preparing them for their twelve month compulsory military service. Then the boy scouts, the girl scouts, even a Unify Cyprus contingent, and standing across from me, backlit by the morning sun, Mercini holding Danae, who was waving a little flag; you might think you were living in happier-ever-after Greece.

It wasn't until many meals had passed with Spiros and his family, that I was reminded of something Americans have trouble remembering: many of the world's people of a certain age, like Loula and her brother Thomas, were children in 1940, when the world was at war on their doorstep, some quite literally.

Thomas was ten on the original Ohi Day, and fourteen in August, 1944, the eldest son of five children, a tall boy with long black hair, hurrying across the square in front of the Cathedral of the Three Hierarchs, en route to his house around the corner, hoping to avoid the soldiers. Having completed the highest school on the island at twelve and because movement was restricted during the occupation, Thomas worked as a delivery boy for his tall tailor father, Theodosius, and his beautiful seamstress mother, Matoula, at a time when very few in Skiathos could afford their services.

Greece was four years into the war and the Skiathans by then had an organized resistance, which was being advised by British and American intelligence officers on the mainland. One day in August, based on the importance of the mission and assurances from Allied Intelligence that there would be no reprisals, the resistance on Skiathos captured Uberlieutenant Adler, the German Commander of the Northern Sporades, his small boat and three of his men, who were in the midst of anchoring off the Bourtzi during one of their routine visits to the island.

Thomas once told me how he remembers walking out the door that day to make a delivery, while Loula, then eight years old and in the third grade, was helping her mother wind thread when the bells of the cathedral angrily rang and booming German voices ordered everyone to the waterfront. He told me his father didn't stop to gather anything, as his mother hurried the smaller children out the door and away from the port, all frantically running like frightened animals, Thomas leading Loula by the hand, his father in the rear carrying his youngest, Yiannis, four, and looking over his shoulder, never stopping until high in the mountains above Skiathos, at the shelter of a friend's *kalivi*, which was near the small stone monastery of Agios Haralambos.

Everyone on the island had known of the day's event so, at the port, no one had responded to the announcement. A long moment of silence, then the sound of footsteps down stone steps outside the cathedral and three priests moved into view and stopped in front of ten angry German soldiers, who were standing outside the Café Asvestis on the port. Later, other villagers tell of how, after another moment, ten or twelve townspeople timidly came forward, followed by the Mayor who froze as the soldiers snapped to attention for a Colonel who appeared from the shadows of the Café Asvestis doorway and, ignoring the priests, stopped in front of the Mayor. Almost anyone from the village can recite his exact words: "Tell the people we are going to do something very bad", to which he quietly added "We are going to wipe out Skiathos."

Then, he ordered the soldiers to leave the priests but to take the townspeople to the boats, which left the island. Of those hostages, two were thrown into the open sea and drowned, three died as prisoners of war camps.

Thomas vividly remembers that night, as he and the older

boys and men of the two families lay awake outside the *kalivi*, and Loula and the women with small children lay awake inside, an August Meltemi wind rolled through the western Aegean. For the next nine days it inhibited the avenging German army with their small boats from leaving Volos. As anyone on the island will tell you, on that same night and for the next nine days, at the end of a long, dusty, winding, bumpy mountain trail in the middle of the forest on the uninhabited north side of the island, men from the village had been working on the oldest monastery on Skiathos dedicated to the Virgin Mary, established in 1350, the Panayia at Kechria, in anticipation of the monastery's Name Day, giving the tiny stone monastery a fresh coat of pink paint on its plaster dome, painting grey steps below a rusted ageless old bell which hung on a chain. In the small clean courtyard with its view to the Aegean, the men would pause and listen for the Germans, as they drank from a constant trickle of clear spring water from a pipe, using a yellow child's cup in the shape of an elephant hanging on a nail. Inside the church, with its exquisite eighteenth century frescoes badly in need of restoration, the floor would be swept, the icons dusted and the monastery, all but forgotten for the rest of the year, would be solemnly remembered on her name day with candles and flowers, occupation or not. Early in the morning of that ninth day, with barely enough food for another day, Thomas remembers how he and his father were returning from another monastery, Evangelistria, where islanders had been leaving fruits and vegetables from their gardens for general distribution and, passing a trickling of townspeople on their way back to Skiathos, his father decided it was possible Allied Intelligence was right, perhaps the Germans would not retaliate. Then he cautiously guided the family back down the mountain to their home in the village, where they uneasily resumed their life. The next night, just after midnight on August 23th, the beginning of the Name Day of the Monastery of the

Panayia at Kechria, the windstorm suddenly stopped and the
Germans immediately set sail for Skiathos.

Before dawn the next morning, as Skiathan lookouts lit
fires to alert the villagers, the German army quickly landed
and completely surrounded the village. Loula described to me
how at 3:30 a.m. they were jarred awake by a loud rap on the
door from their neighbor, Asvestis, the café owner, who was
screaming:

"Go away! Go away!"

Afraid that he looked old enough to be a soldier, Thomas remembers his father grabbing him and running out into
the pitch-black street. Slowly, carefully they moved for several
heart-pounding minutes while they heard voices in the dark.
Then suddenly from behind, a gravel voice in Greek:

"*Alt! Psila ta heria!*" (Stop! Put your hands up!)

"From Volos!" Theodosius recognized the accent, "Collaborator!" Thomas remembers how his father then leaned into him
and whispered, "Run away! Back home! Go!"

Thomas took off towards the cemetery, Theodosius ran in
the opposite direction.

Sudden gunshots! Automatic fire! Running, tripping in the
darkness, crawling on hands and knees, the sound of bullets
scraping stones, Thomas frantically raced past a house, then
ducked into an olive grove and hid behind trees, as the shooting intensified and multiplied all through the village. People
running, screaming, crying. Chaos and confusion reigned in
the narrow streets as Thomas ran towards the cemetery, blinded
by tears, stopping to listen, checking every corner, when out of
the blackness three armed men, two of them Greek cried out:

"*Alt! Psila ta heria!*"

Loula told me that during that time she sat with Matoula
and her sisters in the house in the dark, terrified, listening to
the gunshots and screams. She couldn't stop shaking.

On the port, inside Café Asvestis, were a mother and her

ten-year-old daughter, sobbing, Thomas recalled to me how the Greeks were yelling at him as he was roughly pushed inside.

"Where's the commander!"

"Where are the rebels hiding!?"

One soldier grabbed the little girl, "We're going to kill you!"

The German and the two Greeks pushed the terrified Thomas, the mother and little girl out of the café and down the waterfront towards the Bourtzi, where they were ordered to stop. Thomas told me that as they held each other's hands, two soldiers with machine guns suddenly pointed at them and pulled their triggers. Thomas saw the fire from the muzzles as he closed his eyes and heard the bullets streaming just above his head. He soiled his pants, as did the mother and daughter. Another long blast. The three stood, hands gripped to one other. After a long moment, they were shoved back towards the café, where fifty or sixty older men, women, and children, including Matoula, with her daughters, Sofia, sixteen, Evangelia, ten, Loula, and little Yiannis, were sitting paralyzed with fear. Thomas said he quickly joined them, picking up Yiannis, trying to calm the girls when he saw his father pushed through the door, followed by three German officers. As Theodosius took a seat by his family, one officer strolled through the café, checking faces of all the men and boys:

"How old are you? Anyone between sixteen and sixty years old, stand up!"

Thomas remembers that no one stood.

As the officer approached, his father turned and looked into the eyes of his frightened beautiful bride, Matoula, who had married her handsome husband not by arrangement but out of love, then softly squeezed her hand and slowly stood. Loula remembers that two soldiers took her father roughly by the arms and ordered him to follow them. And then somebody screaming. "He's going to be executed!"

She still remembers an endless beat of silence, then the screaming, the never-ending seconds, everyone screaming, then the sound of gunshots and more screaming and crying, until the Colonel entered the café and fired his pistol. Silence, but for a few quiet sobs. Then, the Colonel looked at them coldly and spoke just above a whisper:

"Go away, all of you. In three minutes we will bomb and burn Skiathos."

Then he turned sharply on his heels and left.

Thomas took his mother's hand, Sofia took Loula, and quickly led the family out of the café where a few feet away lying face down they saw their father's lifeless blood soaked body. Thomas remembers how his mother pushed him away and ran to her husband, insisting on taking his body to the church even as two German officers threatened to kill her. He told me how he calmly intervened and firmly took his mother's hand to gently lead her away.

The Germans had already piled mattresses soaked in paraffin in the doorways of the houses and were sitting in their boats about two hundred yards off shore. Thomas was holding Loula and Yiannis while on his way to the *kalivi* near Agios Haralambos, when he first saw the German planes come out of the clouds and indiscriminately drop bombs that appeared to be made of fire. Two hundred houses began burning during the first run when, just as suddenly as the wind had started nine days ago and suddenly stopped just after midnight the night before, a great unpredicted torrent of rain swept the island, which began putting out most of the fires, and which so discouraged the pilots that they stopped bombing and disappeared. Due to the wind delaying the German onslaught until Her monastery's Nameday, and the rain from nowhere magically extinguishing the fire, those who were on Skiathos that day believe with all their hearts that the island's heavenly patron, the Panayia, once again demonstrated Her love and protection of its people from forces beyond their control. But for Thomas and Loula, their mother and their

brothers and sisters, that day would be even more meaning-
ful, forever changing their lives.

Within two months, Greece was freed. The Germans re-
treated by sea and were overcome by Greek and British subma-
rines, which filled the sea and beaches around Skiathos with
dead German bodies for weeks. One week after the bombing,
Thomas sailed for Piraeus to join his uncle, who worked as a
forwarding agent in a shipping company. He enrolled in night
school and began taking English lessons underwritten by the
U.S. Information Office, which would enable him one day to
be the captain of a large luxury liner, sailing the world in a
luxurious cabin with his wife, master of his domain; but for a
whole year after the event, Thomas said that he spent all of his
spare time sitting on a rock by the sea, weeping.

Loula, on the other hand, stayed at home and helped her
mother, until she was twenty-six, an age when she was in
danger of being labeled an old maid. Having already rejected
several candidates, a marriage was arranged to a man she had
never met named Kostas and with whom, during their first
year together, she would fall madly in love, as would Kostas
with Loula. He would go on to become the mayor of Skiathos
and they would live happily for many years. Now a widow and
an orphan, Loula, a handsome woman with silver hair, had
a framed black and white photograph of her handsome husband and one of her father and mother, which would continue
to look over every gathering from the sideboard in her dining
room.

On Ohi Day, I was sitting at that dining table across from
Thomas. Seeing him so at peace, so quick to sing or urge someone to dance, feeling his gentleness, I asked him why I never
sensed the pain and anger he must still feel as a result of that
tragedy. He smiled.

"In 1954, I joined a passenger liner as a cadet, an appren-
tice captain. Among the crew were a hundred and seventy-five

Germans. They treated me like a king. We got along very well. I think it was obvious, they felt sorry. What feeling do I carry from that day? I guess a greater appreciation of life."

How soft was his tone, how accepting of the facts, of the fate, without judgment, even regarding himself, the depth of his pain, and I began to grasp the depth of his character, the hugeness of his spirit, and blushed at the ease and shallowness of my own small life. Perhaps from their ill fortune a greater openness to life and love emerged, which had spilled over to Spiros, Matoula and Mercini, and down again to Danae, in her mother's arms, laughing, waving her flag, standing only a few steps from the spot where her great grandfather, Theodosius, lay executed, where her great uncle Thomas, as a boy, the same age as the boys marching in front of her, carried his little brother, Yiannis, while taking his weeping mother by the hand and urging her and the family away.

Where does his kind of forgiveness come from? Is it necessary to have suffered a great wrong to be able to forgive so totally? Why was it so hard for me to forgive my father for a so much less serious injustice? These thoughts plagued me on my drive home that day.

My father was a prince, being the oldest of six children, being a boy, being the one who taught my illiterate grandfather how to sign his name, being the first in the family, not to mention the first in the whole twelve family Lebanese community in Barre, Vermont, to graduate high school, then on to the university, where he distinguished himself academically and even wrote his fraternity's anthem which is still sung today, then to one of the great medical schools, where he received very good grades his freshman year. Pictures of him during that winter show a short, wide, broadly smiling, curly haired young man in a raccoon coat, in a 1928 convertible. But his life took a turn when during that summer, the medical school informed him he was not being invited to return. Being a prince, it never occurred to him that it wasn't acceptable to be argumentative, challenging, overly confident, or to insinuate that he knew more than his professors. So his American dream was suddenly shattered, the brass ring was taken from his grasp, and after brooding and getting into fistfights in bars for a year, he enrolled in Dental School from which he graduated. In the meantime, a high school mate he had always considered vulgar and beneath him finished medical school and became a well respected orthopedic surgeon and, although my father encouraged people to call him Doc and he had a physician's license plate on his car, he was always reminded that it was his vulgar friend that had grabbed the brass and he only the pewter.

The reaction of a prince to being humiliated and denied is most usually anger and I, unhappily, was the one to become the object of it. My mother thought that of their six sons I was the one most like him and that I challenged him the way he challenged his professors, which unhappily also tested his temper. Being extremely creative, he would also devise thoughtful punishments for me, like painting my fingernails with red nail polish in order to keep me from biting them and then sending me off to school. As a five year old in the first grade I was a spirited boy, so I scraped the polish off with my teeth before entering the schoolyard and no one was the wiser. Of course, when my father returned home from work that day, the first thing he did was to order me to show him my nails. Which I did. He shook his head then promptly went to a closet, opened his tool box, took out a hammer, held my fingers to the table and dropped the hammer on each of my nails. The pain was excruciating. The next morning, he repainted my sore fingernails and again sent me off to school. This time, however, I snuck into Woolworth's Five and Dime and stole a similar red nail polish, then scraped my nails clean again before I entered the schoolyard. Although I had difficulty writing that day, no one

was the wiser. On the way home, I repainted my nails with the
stolen polish. They looked perfect. Of course, when my father
came home that day after work, he again ordered me to show
him my nails, which I did, confidently. He stared at them a long
moment, moving them in and out of the light. Then, he threw
me a look and strode into his bedroom, grabbed my mother's
nail polish off their dresser, brought it to me, and painted one
of my nails. As we watched it dry, we both realized at the same
moment that the reds were slightly different. Hoping against
hope that I would at least be praised for my ingenuity, I wasn't
surprised when my father, not impressed, threw me a seriously
ugly look, then retrieved his hammer from the closet and once
again dropped it on my poor little digits, then painted them
again before he sent me off to school the next morning.

One of the great regrets in life is the inability through death
or distance to know certain adults as an adult. He died age
fifty-five when I was twenty-one. Had he lived longer, perhaps
I might have had an easier time forgiving him. He might have
even mellowed and I might have seen him more clearly in context and been less challenging. But when his life ended, my
relationship with him froze in anger, and I spent my entire
adult life searching for a substitute, while deploring in myself
so many of his unattractive traits.

I'd always been considered an angry man, an injustice collector, collecting slights, real or imagined. Sins of the father
was my apologia. You beat a dog he becomes angry. Actors for
the most part will tell you they had a bad father-son relationship. It may be what drove them to act, to look for approval
from a director, who would become in effect a surrogate father.
I used to play my father when I was playing villains. I could
feel what it felt like for my father, and when I would watch my
angry twisted face on the screen, it was the face of my father.
Perhaps it was a way to get to know him, by becoming him. As
we pulled into our driveway, I decided to take time to examine

why after so long I still couldn't forgive him. New friends were shaming me into facing old demons.

When I arrived home, I went to our box of photographs, hunting for a black and white professional photo taken of him on the occasion of the announcement of his dental practice. I had seen the photo a thousand times, yet never really looked at it, at him, and was struck dumb when I realized that, in place of the confidence, even cockiness that I had remembered, what I saw was a young man with a deep sadness in his eyes, the look of a man tired of being himself, of all the disappointments, and I suddenly wished that he was on Skiathos, living downstairs like Loula does with Spiros and Matoula, and we could sit on the terrace just once and drink wine, and I could tell him that it was all right. I put his picture in a silver frame on our piano where, together with the rest of our family and friends, he would look out over every gathering.

Proust writes about waking up in the morning without the faintest clue of your death in the afternoon, or how your day would really end. Mine would end lighter than it started. Forgiving was not so hard. Maybe the last part of your life was supposed to be spent in love and forgiveness. These were my thoughts as I stepped outside with my binoculars to watch the ferry returning to Volos, having been to the outer islands, Skopelos, Alonnisos, sailing the same channel Xerxes sailed with his fleet twenty-five hundred years ago. This small country, such history, such heart! I felt great pride for my newly adopted people and I thought how much my father also would have loved Greece, and suddenly I blurted into tears and cried so hard Anthea later asked me what I had been singing.

QUIET TIME

There is a fullness of all things, even of sleep and of love.

Homer

With November's Indian summer the days became shorter and cooler and, with the exception of a week of rain and a few cold snaps, autumn continued until well after the new year. Like the leafless fig trees and grape vines, the island was pared down to its bare limbs, the actual Skiathans, who by birth or by choice once again became the traditional fishermen and small farmers. There was a renewed intimacy on the island, a sigh of relief that the madness was over, and in its place the stillness needed to perfectly prune an olive tree.

After the first rain, all the island's greenery, as well as the small seasonal hotel gardens with their geraniums and roses around Koukounaries had been cleansed and refreshed and were vibrant. Chestnut and sycamore trees were golden, the maples a brilliant red, and pomegranates hung like crimson Christmas balls amid thin bright golden leaves. Hillsides of dried heather appeared on fire in the sun, clusters of yellow daisies suddenly sprouted among the olive trees, berries were out in abundance, from alabaster to black, and the entire color spectrum in between, all sizes from jawbreakers to B.B.'s, bird food for the great migration's rest stop at middle earth, from everywhere north to everywhere south, altogether a blend of fall which, together with the crunch of leaves underfoot, reminded me of my boyhood in Vermont. The air was crisp and clean, and all the colors were clearer and deeper. More and more time was spent just watching the ever-changing sky, from searing pink sunrises to wine dark sea sunsets, occasionally so wildly dramatic Anthea would look up and shake her head:

"Now He's gone too far."

Some Skiathans, especially the ones enslaved by the tourist industry, had harvested their olives and made their wine and had now left the island for their vacations, either south to loll on a beach, or north, skiing. Some ex pats, like Roy and Jane, had left to shop. Some left simply to get away from the sameness of their lives. But the events of the last year and a half required such enormous energy, the only thing Anthea and I were craving was quiet. Being surrounded by such beauty and such serenity, constantly, other than our trip to the Peloponnesus, it never occurred to us to leave even for a moment. I still hadn't gotten "island fever", which surprised me. On vacation in Hawaii, I'd begin to feel anxious after the first week. Anthea said it was because in Hawaii, when I looked out, all I saw was water, which intensified the feeling, whereas on Skiathos, because it was surrounded by so much land from neighboring islands and the mainland, it felt more like being on a lake. Most of the expatriates who were retired and couldn't afford to travel, complained about the coming winter: too cold and rainy, nothing to do. I felt for them. Left alone with nothing you have to do and nothing to do, what do you do? And when you have nothing you have to do and nothing to do for an extended period of time, like winter, what then? Bruce had warned us about the winters on a small island, that we would have to be self directed, otherwise we'd be reduced to driving down to the port to watch the ferry come in, a ritual I rather happened to enjoy. I had the same concerns, but I also wondered what would happen if I left myself alone and allowed something outside myself to affect me, perhaps even direct me. Maybe a passion would emerge, one I might not even know existed but had been lurking beneath the veneer of my old life.

I was pondering that question one afternoon, while walking around Koukounaries in the quiet. Since I wasn't concerned about accomplishing anything anymore and now had the luxury of worry-free, task-free use of my mind, coupled with a thousand daily indulgences like pausing to watch the ducks by Strofilia Pond, I was quite comfortable setting the question aside for a moment and simply letting the air filter through my brain, along with the melody of a Greek folk song, while meandering down the narrow winding road away from the beach. Passing underneath a pair of large maples, the damp autumn colors, the cold, the musty smell, the leaves underfoot, I had a moment like Proust when he tasted the tea-soaked madeleine. Suddenly, I was six and wore thick glasses and Simone, a chubby pretty blond, had reluctantly asked me to our second grade "Girls' Choice" dance at St. Monica's Elementary School. I liked her and was thrilled to be there, dancing the box step, having never been so close to a girl before, let alone Simone, whose fleshy neck glistened with tiny beads of sweat, while Sister Matthew walked around the room sliding her hand between couples:

"Remember, the Holy Ghost must dance between you!"

Having to pee, and badly, in the middle of what seemed like an endless song, and not knowing how to excuse myself in the middle without appearing stupid to my little snow angel, I continued dancing, even inventing new moves, waiting for the record to end until I finally peed in my grey wool pants, and for the rest of the afternoon, which for us ended early, neither acknowledged there was a strong smell of urine on wool, coming from a stain the size of a melon around my crotch. Simone was very gracious and well deserving of my adoration, but after that cold walk home together, when the only sound from either of us was the crunch of leaves underfoot and the wet of my pants, which had frozen and were rubbing against my thighs, I would never look her in the eye again. Now in an instant, on that road, I felt that moment so vividly and I shuddered when it struck me, this profoundly embarrassing moment, this sore in my psyche that I had been carrying since I was six, was in fact a tender, sweet moment of innocence, something to be treasured, celebrated. Then I was reminded of the brilliance of Plato's maxim "The life unexamined is not worth living", and I realized that up until now I'd been so busy living and learning and earning and doing that I hadn't had the leisure to look back and examine, for instance, other profoundly embarrassing moments. Perhaps they would all in hindsight be at worst charming. But I soon ran into several that no amount of contextualizing, rationalizing, or spinning mitigated from being anything other than profoundly shameful and embarrassing and better left undisturbed.

The melody of the folk song was creeping back into my brain as I reached the horse farm. Newly seeded grass had already begun to sprout in the pasture. On the pond side of the road, two old women in black were stooped over, picking wild greens among the short-stemmed flowers, to be used as medicinal herbs in the winter. Old women often walked far from the village for these gatherings, then hitchhiked back. I always enjoyed giving them a ride. I was taken aback at first when I realized we were around the same age. I had always thought of them as old. I also felt so much younger than they looked, and I wondered if they also felt much younger than they looked in their black dresses and kerchiefs. At first, they spoke in Greek with a casual familiarity. They were surprised when I couldn't understand them. I looked Greek to them. They blamed Anthea for not teaching me. It was her fault. Why would I argue? The truth was that I was beginning to get a sense of the language. I now knew the alphabet and could sound out words and was surprised how many I recognized, like *epigrafi*, epigraph or sign, *micro*, small. People were encouraging, and every time I would introduce a new Greek word at the bank, for instance, to tall and elegant Kiki, one of the tellers, she and the bank manager would quietly clap and cheer.

Koukounaries Beach was wrapped tight for the winter. The sand was firm to walk on, the water clear and clean and still. I picked up a few softball-size pinecones for kindling. Where a few months ago it had been lined with umbrellas and bathers, it was now only me, and where a half dozen yachts, some of considerable size, had been anchored in the bay, there was one small orange and blue Greek fishing boat, a one man operation, laying a net just off the shore, trapping the small fish sold in the fish market by the port or off the boat itself. I stopped at one of the green wooden benches under the large pines and sat charmed by the timeless scene.

You could now park on Papadiamanti Street, whereas twelve weeks ago there was hardly elbow room. Everyone but Geof suddenly had time for the leisurely coffee or ouzo. He was always in a hurry, ex hippie, rushing to meet someone. After months and months of excuses, Anthea began painting. Lemons. It had been a long time since she failed at anything, and she wasn't confident. She originally wanted to be a painter but quit in her twenties, because she felt she could never be as good as Matisse. After a dozen still lifes, fruits, vegetables and flowers, Anthea declared herself a talented amateur.

"It's a good start", I told her.

Spiros gave her a book of Fayum paintings, portraits from the second century from a colony of Greeks in Fayum Egypt, who painted exquisite soulful faces on wood, the earliest expressionists, a school Anthea had been drawn to before she quit painting, and which were now slowly seducing her back. In the meantime, she was still working on a fine green pear, although

Maria's favorite was the orange, because it looked real enough to eat.

I planted several dozen roses and fruit and nut trees, nearly everything that could grow in Greece, from cherries and walnuts to lemons and quince. After digging the hole for the first of the trees, a peach, I was laying down my shovel when Maria, carrying a basket of laundry, paused to watch. After a moment, she put down her load, picked up the shovel and quickly, wordlessly, and with surprising strength dug out my hole, which was slightly larger than the tree container, until it was perhaps a yard by two feet. Then, grabbing the tree from my hand, she judo chopped off its plastic container, relaxed its cramped roots as she lowered it into the hole, and shoveled in the proper mixture of dirt and goat manure, the latter which had just been delivered in a large dump truck. Handing me the shovel with a look, she stomped around the tree, creating a bowl to hold the water, then scooped up her laundry and continued on her way. I then realized why the baby fruit trees I had planted in Hollywood, although healthy, remained exactly the same size for twenty years.

The days seemed to pass quickly, and when all the trees were planted and the roses and grapes goat-manured, I waited and prayed for a night of light rain, the sound of drops on the roof and windows, soaking my precious little babies, my new responsibilities, living things with which I would now have a lifelong relationship, grooming and feeding them and promising them health care in return for their exquisite fruit, my garden in Eden. It was a good feeling, a great feeling watching my garden grow. I felt no compelling need to achieve. No reason to feel timid about putting down a book for twenty minutes to watch two butterflies court on a cloudless day. Nothing to do but be. Yet, I was growing as well. For the first time in my life I would not have any trouble answering the question, "What do you do all day?"

"What did Adam and Eve do all day?" I would have to answer.

I knew it was an important question for those whose drive to continually succeed was habitual, one I sincerely tried to answer until the day I realized that if you had to ask the question, you probably weren't ready to hear the answer.

When it finally did rain, it was in the early morning. I stood under the eave outside the kitchen door and let the drops wash my hand. It was a gentle rain, quiet. Perfect for my new young friends. Autumn, it seemed, was unfolding as it should.

KOUNISTRA

Time will explain it all.

Euripides

During my life in Hollywood I always marvelled at a film crew, a group that could build almost anything in practically no time, tear it down in less, and move on. Everyone had a job and every job was important to the whole, like a well tuned orchestra, and everyone knew and enjoyed the value of their contribution. Every principal actor was assigned a car and driver who was sensitive to his charge. If they wanted quiet, there was quiet. If they wanted to laugh, he had ready a litany of jokes, knowing his performance would affect the actors in theirs.

On Skiathos, in much the same way, I soon realized everyone made a contribution, and every contribution was important in maintaining the harmony and well-being of the small island community. Like the sirto, everyone held hands and weaved their way through the day, and like the dance, there was always room for one more, and anyone at any time could take the lead, even Jimmy, with his flat facial profile, small ears and upwardly slanted eyes, who ran errands and did odd jobs for his brother at the fish market near the port.

Born forty-five years ago with Down Syndrome, Jimmy, all dressed up in his brown suit and red tie, was always applauded as he unofficially led every parade, was always on the bandstand

at every official public gathering and was traditionally paid 20
euros by the villagers to carry the lid of the coffin at every funeral procession as it wound its way through the village streets
to the cemetery, all of which the Skiathans did cheerfully, casually, without regard for any blessings they might earn for their
kindness. It was part of what made the people on this small
island all step together.

In the middle of a sunny November afternoon, while resting at the bottom of our property under a very old chestnut
tree amidst a spray of wild purple crocuses, I was fingering
the nuts I had just finished picking, my first basket, and I had
been thinking of Jimmy and the sweet harmony the islanders
enjoyed, which by pure luck we happened to stumble upon,
when I could hear the faint sound of laughter and chatter coming from the dirt road in the valley below. My friend Mihalis
told me to expect that on this day, from our house, we would
see the islanders on their way to the Monastery of the Virgin
Kounistra. From behind a hill, groups were emerging; some
just couples, others in large extended families, their children
playing as they ran along the road ahead. It was Thanksgiv-
ing Day in Skiathos, the day Skiathans honored their goddess,
their patron saint, the Panayia, who protected them and granted them the bounty they received over the year.

As Mihalis explained to me, people on neighboring Skopelos Island believed that because Skiathans didn't have their own
patron saint, like their Agios Riginos, the miracle of Kounistra
was born. But most Skiathans believed that in 1655, a virtu-
ous old Skiathan hermit monk named Simeon, while praying in his tiny *kalivi*, saw a bright light shining high, deep in
the forest, as if a star had fallen to earth. He tried with great
persistence and with much prayer and fasting to find it, but
each time the light would vanish until just before dawn on the
feast day in Greek Orthodoxy, which celebrated the Virgin at
twelve years old, being first taken to serve in the temple. All

that night, Simeon had followed the light as it kept appearing and disappearing until, in the middle of the thickest part of the forest, where no one ever wandered, the light finally revealed itself to him: an exceptionally fine Byzantine icon of the Virgin, her eyes looking slightly to her left, her lips stern as if she were keeping a watchful eye. Hanging high on the tallest branch of a huge pine tree, the mysterious icon was spinning and swaying in the wind, reflecting the moonlight. Believing it was a miracle, Simeon knelt and prayed until morning when, witnessed by the chief priests and community leaders of Skiathos, the youngest priest on the island climbed to the top of the eighty foot tree and retrieved it.

They called it Eikon Astria, the icon of the star, and since no one could explain its origin or how it happened to be up so high in that huge pine tree in the middle of a forest that no one ever entered, only to be discovered on her feast day, it was believed by all assembled to be a sign from the Virgin that the Skiathans would be her children and under her parental care. The island had its patron saint.

The priests took the icon to Simeon's chapel, which gradually expanded and became known as the Monastery of Virgin Kounistra, as the icon became revered not only because of its magical origin but for its miraculous ability to cure brain disorders of any kind, whether psychological or physical, including paralysis and epilepsy. As word spread of the icon's power, people from all over the Mediterranean made pilgrimages to petition the Virgin.

In 1852, due to frequent raids by pirates, the icon was taken from her monastery and placed in the Cathedral of the Three Hierarchs in the village for safekeeping. Since then, for over one hundred and fifty years, at one o'clock on the anniversary of the day before Simeon discovered the icon, the church bells in Skiathos ring and hundreds assemble at the cathedral square where the icon, now framed in polished silver and gold

which is itself framed in elaborately carved wood, is taken from
her secure place in the cathedral and carried in solemn procession up the stone steps to a second parish church, the Panayia
Lymnias, where more people are waiting and another service is
held. After that service, the procession, which includes a dozen
priests, altar boys and the church choir, is joined by the Skiathos
Philharmonic Band in their crisp military uniforms and moves
solemnly down the hill to the acropolis amid firecracker explo-
sions and the firing of shotguns, as the police watch amused.
At the acropolis, many more hundreds of people, all carrying
an abundance of food and drink, gather for yet another short
service, after which the procession continues to the edge of the
village where the band marches in place and plays as the icon
and townspeople continue out of town and onto an ancient
footpath. Some, who have special requests of the Virgin, walk
barefoot on the three hour journey through the center of the island, up and down two mountains to the Panayia's monastery.

Mihalis also told me that for as many years, young children
in their innocence had claimed to see the Virgin smiling as she
approached her monastery and her eyes wet with tears as she
was carried away from her home and back to the cathedral the
next morning, but he never saw such smiles or tears as a child
and didn't believe in the miracle of the icon anyway.

On the road below, the large procession had paused. As in
most of the island's celebrations, almost everyone would be
there: Nikos the druggist, hoping today would be the day he
would meet his future wife, Popi from the toy store with her
sweetly smiling daughter Effie, another of our bank tellers,
many Mitzelos families, some of whom would not be speaking
to each other.

There was a sudden burst of laughter, then another. I
couldn't imagine what was so funny but it became infectious
and I found myself laughing, alone, half way up the mountain,
feeling a little of what it must be like to be a God. But the

laughter quickly evaporated as Papa Yiorgos began chanting and the choir sang and Papa Nikolas swung the censor. After several hymns, the group began the long walk up the winding road to the top of the second mountain, chatting and laughing.

By the time the icon arrived at the monastery, Anthea and I had already parked the jeep and had walked through the grounds filled with families unpacking sleeping bags and pitching tents. Finding a space on a fieldstone wall in the courtyard, we spread a small blanket and set down a picnic basket we had bought for the event. The service that followed was solemn. Since the church was quite small, everyone stepped in for a moment then stepped out again to make room for another.

While the service continued, bonfires were lit and families began eating mezethes and drinking ouzo and wine. After lighting a candle, Anthea and I returned to our blanket with our cold supper. The mayor stopped to greet us as well as others, including my neighbor Yiorgos, who insisted on sharing his wife's cheese pie. After the service, there was singing and dancing in what would be an all night vigil.

The priests, the altar boys and the choir with their families, all remained and everyone danced, even Jimmy who, astonishingly, danced with uncommon grace, like a creature clumsy on land but utterly well designed for water.

Anthea and I joined the sirto, which coiled through the courtyard, until my legs gave out. Anthea, on the other hand, having complained earlier in the day about a sore hip, seemed to find it no impediment to dancing with the abandon of a gypsy. The legend of the icon, the service, the whole celebration seemed to strike a vibrant chord in her, and as I sat on the wall and watched her, I was reminded of all the nights she would arrive home from working as a film executive. Dropping her script satchel en route to the stove, she would immediately start dinner for Robert and me without even bothering to take off her outer coat, until the onions were chopped and on the fire, checking Robert's homework as she basted a chicken or strained a vegetable, always taking her usual great care with every chore. Now, filled with such joy in this firelight, she was stepping and stamping and bending with an unending reserve of energy, at different times the six year old, the teen aged temptress, the decisive, powerful woman, confident of her sexuality. There was a new freedom in her movement, and as I watched I began musing that one of the collateral rewards of a long marriage was seeing the layers of inhibition gradually peel away over time, revealing the other in their fullness, unearthing the child that you had been living with, but which you were only allowed to get to know according to how much this "child" trusted you. Anthea always claimed she had been born an adult and in fact could speak in simple sentences even before she could walk. But over the years, I began to suspect she had simply hidden the child from the world, especially in her particular childhood when, if you asked a Greek man how many children he had, he might answer two, and also one daughter. Now, as I watched her take a turn at the lead, after so many years of pretending to be an adult, I suspected that the little girl who was called Anthoula by her family was finally making her debut. Just then, a woman in her sixties, small and strong with a red face that could be related to Santa Claus, took Anthea's hand and became the lead. Argyro. Everyone knew her. She was born in Skiathos. Her father had been a fisherman but nobody ever remembered seeing him. He went to sea when Argyro was in grade school and never returned. Later, it became apparent that he abandoned the family after he learned his wife, although still a young woman, had contracted Parkinson's Disease, leaving her with seven children to beg in the streets until her early death at fifty-two. Argyro couldn't go to high school, even though it existed at that time. She had to work to help feed her brothers and sisters after her mother's death. At thirteen, she began cleaning houses. After being married and divorced with three children, Argyro, still a young woman, continued cleaning houses, but work became increasingly irregular as Albanians began arriving to do the same work for less money, and since she wasn't trained to do anything else, it became increasingly difficult for her to provide for herself and her children.

"I had as many problems as the grains of sand on Koukounaries", she confided to me one day.

It was then she prayed to the Virgin for help. One of the responsibilities of the mayor in Skiathos was to keep a paternal eye on vulnerable Skiathans when doling out political appointments. Sixteen years ago, it was the trim, balding, cigar smoking pediatrician who, when the opportunity arose, appointed Argyro guardian of the monastery. There would be no salary, just room and donations, mostly from candles. The life would be Spartan, but the present would be secure and, after a life of strife and struggle, the future assured. Argyro, ever grateful, was convinced she was singled out by the Virgin, and would work at the Monastery of the Panayia Kounistra indefatigably, joyously.

If custody of the important old monastery had been awarded for chastity, Argyro never would have qualified. More like the legend of Mary Magdalene than the Virgin she served, Argyro had been known to sing and dance utterly uninhibited on nights other than this, and even point to some much younger man:

"I want you tonight, Vasilis!"

But after having singly scoured and scrubbed, swept and polished, pruned, and planted tirelessly, preparing the monastery for this event while fasting for twenty-one days, without meat, fish, cheese, or milk, and for the last days no oil, and during that whole time dressed only in black, on this night she traditionally loosened all the screws. This had always been her favorite holiday anyway, and she was always determined not to let it pass quietly; but by the time she would be dancing seductively on a table, Anthea and I would be fast asleep.

In the morning, I was waiting at my perch half way up the mountain when about noon, I heard the first laughter and chatter as the Skiathans began returning. An hour after the icon passed, Anthea, deeply exhausted, was still asleep, so I drove down to the village alone and stood with a crowd of people on Papadiamanti Street and watched the procession, which had again been joined by the Skiathos Philharmonic Band, and smiling, leading the procession, was Jimmy, the icon sitting high on his hunched right shoulder, lumbering his way to the cathedral. I couldn't say for certain there was a tear in the Virgin's eye as she passed by me, but I couldn't say there wasn't. I did notice tears in several of the children's eyes, however, when Jimmy handed the Panayia to Papa Yiorgos, who took the Virgin inside and set her in her place to be undisturbed for another year.

'TIS THE SEASON

I grow old ever learning many things.

Solon

During the first week in December, yellow and white lights in snowflake shapes were draped over Papadiamanti Street, twinkling white lights had been wound around the mulberry trees and old style street lamps, and skiff-size shells of Greek sail boats suddenly appeared outlined in lights in the front yards of houses. Originally the symbol of Dionysius, who was the island's ancient patron, boats were now the traditional Christmas tree. Along the quay, twinkling lights were now hanging on the tavernas, while near the Bourtzi, lighting up the harbor, the outline of a thirteen sail Greek merchant ship covered in white lights, the kind of ship Skiathans were renowned for building in the 18th century. The days were getting shorter, and what began as the ancient pagan festival of lights to woo the sun back from its retreat into the heavens was a welcome relief.

On Christmas Eve morning, Anthea awoke and for the first time in our thirty years together announced she wanted to go to church. I pretended not to be surprised. For the rest of the day, I resisted asking the obvious question, and after dinner we dressed, wordlessly, and drove to the village for the midnight mass.

The cathedral was filled to overflowing. Inside there were many more women and children than men, who only stepped inside to light a few candles, then stepped back out and milled about or sat on a marble bench whose back was the cathedral's outer wall, chatting and smoking, waiting for their wives. It was startling to see someone who you met every day in work clothes, with hair slightly disheveled, dressed in a blue suit and tie or a dress and high heels. It seemed the whole village had gathered. So many candles were being lit for so many intentions, that a small, wiry old man stopped by the table every fifteen or twenty minutes, scooping out half-burnt very thin candles from the back of the tray in one swift motion, using both hands, and blowing them out and replacing the ones from the back with the lighted ones in the front, in order to make room for the next group.

After entering the cathedral, Anthea and I lit several candles. Then Anthea moved to a series of icons, kissing each one, and slipped behind a row of chairs where she stood, hands folded, listening to the priest and choir exchange responses in the age old language once so familiar to her:

"Ayios O Theos, Ayios Iskiros, Agios Athanatos, Eleison imas", Holy God, Holy and Strong, Holy and Immortal, have mercy on us.

In Greece, the Christmas season begins on Saint Nicholas' Nameday, December 6th, and ends on January 6th, the Epiphany, which was Christ's Baptism in the river Jordan. For most Skiathans, Christmas still had much more Christ than kitsch and was a religious holiday, which meant fasting since mid November, no meat, and for Spiros, ever traditional, no dairy until December 25th. The day was actually established as the birth of Christ by Emperor Constantine in the 2nd century, stretching facts to find common points between Christian and Pagan holidays to make the transition to Christianity less problematic. For Pagans, December 25th was Mithra, the Day of the Invincible Sun, symbolizing the increase of daylight. Children in Greece then, holding a model ship in honor of the god Dionysius, as now, holding a triangle which symbolizes the Trinity and which also supplies the rhythm, knocked on neighbors' doors and shouted, *Na ta poume*, shall we sing, and have sung essentially the same carol uninterrupted for over two thousand years, wishing the landlord and his wife a blessing from the divinity and a long life in return for a coin and a sweet. The real Saint Nicholas was born on December 6th in the 3rd century in what is now Turkey. Following Jesus' notion of charity, the Byzantine Bishop of Myra, always depicted in the traditional red robe of Bishops, used his inheritance anonymously in the service of the least fortunate. It is said he once furnished the dowries for three penniless girls, who could not otherwise have married and probably would have been sold into slavery, by throwing bags of gold through their open window as he walked by and which, as legend has it, landed in their stockings hung by the hearth to dry. A man of extraordinary character and power, known as the friend and protector of all in trouble or need, he became patron saint of sailors and voyagers in the Byzantine world, having once been on a ship during a mighty storm which threatened to capsize the vessel when he knelt and prayed, while the terrified sailors watched in amazement as the wind and waves suddenly calmed.

Santa Claus was born in Manhattan around 1822 with the help of Clement Clark Moore's poem A Visit From Saint Nicholas, relocating Saint Nicholas' Name Day of December 6th to December 25th and his home to the North Pole. His inspiration was the new fallen snow he could see from his study window, complete with sleighs on the road below. And yet, knowing Christ wasn't really born on Christmas and Santa Claus was from Turkey, we still perpetuate the myths, historical fiction passing off as fact, and as I sat on the bench outside the cathedral in the cold, confused and sleepy, I wondered if it was because we all want to believe someone might walk by and throw bags of gold through our window.

From inside the church, the joyous songs of Saint Romanos the Melodist, Byzantium's most celebrated hymnist from 5th century Syria, echoed in the square. Keeping me awake was the fact that my real surname was Romanos and that I changed it to Romanus as a young actor to keep from being typecast a Latino, whose roles were limited. In addition, I was a Lebanese Maronite Christian, whose ancestors were forced to migrate from Syria to Lebanon in the 6th century, after trying to mediate a schism between the Roman and Byzantine churches with their own new compromise creed. Coupling these with the fact that my whole family was rather musical, it made me wonder, and I was feeling a cautious pride as I listened to the glorious music of a possible relative.

As the mass continued inside, I became vaguely aware of an old woman sitting outside the arch of the church, begging, her palm open and offered to each of the faithful as they entered, dressed in black, her face so wrinkled and worn, easily older than any woman there; and almost without exception the people entering consistently gave, if not generously, at least a coin, to which she graciously thanked them. I only had a 20 euro bill, so donating was out of the question until, finally, after seeing almost everyone press something into her palm as they entered and left, and ashamed of my miserliness together with feeling the guilt of so privileged and glorious a life, I folded the bill and slipped it in her hand. At first, she was stunned that it was paper, which I must admit made me feel rather magnanimous. Then, as her glance revealed the size of the bill, tears flooded her eyes and I half expected her to turn into a swan or a beautiful maiden or something mythical, but she grasped my hand and spoke a flood of Greek, which by gesture and word I understood she wanted me to know she was begging to eat. I was touched. She kissed my hand. I put my palm on her cheek and kissed her forehead. As I started into the cathedral she stopped me. In her hand she held an old key chain with a small icon attached, which she kissed and handed to me with a few more words, which I assumed was her blessing. It was perhaps the most satisfying 20 euros I've ever spent and I was suddenly catapulted into the real spirit of Christmas. As I slipped back inside the church to get Anthea's attention, I was startled to see the most unsentimental creature ever created standing in the crowd, not tall enough to see anything but the back of the woman in front, singing full throated along with the choir, tears streaming down her face, obviously overcome, a complete surprise, her own madelaine moment, the mass, the language, the incense, all bringing her back to standing so small between her father, whose elegant bearing she would imitate, and her grandmother, Maria, who only spoke Greek and thought anyone who couldn't must be stupid, and who convinced Anthea until she was seven that if something good happened to them somewhere a Turk must have died. And now they were gone and it was like being among them again, and the flood of that moment tore a hole in an old wall and, just like when Guido found his bark, Anthea rediscovered a part of herself she thought had ceased to exist.

Whether it was because of that mass I couldn't be certain but, around that time, more and more music began flowing through her: singing with the radio while cooking, quietly humming to herself while playing on the computer, while walking, riding, doing almost any chore, although her favorite was to sing while I played the piano to her favorite Theodorakis song, *Sorrow*:

You don't know what cold is
Night without the moon
Not recognizing at what moment
The pain will overtake you

After the midnight mass, Christmas dinner was in the old section of the village on the edge of a bluff overlooking the sea, at the home where Spiros had grown up. He greeted us warmly at the door, took our coats and ushered us into a large room filled with art, antiques and treasures passed down through generations, a home of substance and history. Two large tables were set, one for the children of all ages, one for the adults. Spiros' cousin, Takis, had donated two of his turkeys, and Spiros slaughtered one of his pigs, an ancient custom in itself. The pig was hung to dry for a day and a half, then skinned. The fat was boiled into a liquid and would be used as a sealant for all things which needed to be made water resistant, from shoes to boats and outdoor furniture. Takis' niece, Oriana, made the traditional Christmas melt-in-your-mouth pork with celery, and nobody walked through the door without something baked, except us. This was a family who enjoyed their own recipes with their own secret ingredients, so we sent flowers and brought wine.

Spiros was enjoying breaking his five week fast and was eating slowly and deliberately while bemoaning the fact that some of the young people had stopped following the tradition, the long fast, the joyous church service unchanged since the 4th century, then the walk back through the village in the dark, tired and hungry from the fast, where the smell of pork cooking in fireplaces was all over the island and the meal filled you with a rare happiness. To miss that meant missing something your ancestors had shared with their ancestors, traditions handed down for good reason, for health, for the spirit, as a way of teaching values to the children, and even, as during the long centuries of occupation, a way of reaffirming their identity.

On New Year's Eve day, the sun was shining in a clear sky and I needed no more than a sweater while walking down Papadiamanti Street to get the papers. Everyone was greeting each other with *"Kali chronia"*, Happy New Year, shops were closing and I had to step aside to let the Skiathos Philharmonic Band march by as they continued up and down the street several times playing carols. Clusters of small children were walking around in Sunday clothes with their triangles, knocking on doors singing:

"Saint Basil is coming!"

The children believe that on New Year's Eve Saint Basil visits their house, blesses their family, their belongings and animals, and leaves them presents, placing them on their pillow while they sleep. As a result of Greek Orthodox politics, St. Basil, Byzantium's greatest teacher during a time when heresies were running rampant, in order to strengthen his status, was given all the characteristics of St. Nicholas and subsequently of Santa Claus, who first arrived in Greece only a few decades ago in a Coca Cola commercial. The black-bearded, tall, gaunt, dark skinned Levantine with a deeply furrowed brow and long nose became the jolly, white bearded, fur-suited gift giver from the North Pole.

In Skiathos, since there is no tradition of celebrating at midnight on New Year's Eve, the ex pats usually find a taverna, and those who can stay up sing Auld Lang Syne at midnight. Anthea and I had joined Geof and Lida and the Hunts for dinner for twelve at a taverna in the village, which a century ago was a general store where they say Papadiamantis came every day for an ouzo, one olive, and a handful of pistachios. Of the twelve this night, eight of us were Americans, including a couple from New York City, science and media nonfiction writers who, being in Italy on a book tour in the early summer, came to Skiathos for a two week holiday and never left, and were writing their next book in a small house in the village, using the Internet for research. Much of the conversation was how different the United States looked from here, and how increasingly our homeland was isolating itself from the larger world and without the greater population realizing how profound the change. At the stroke of midnight, having

already paid the check, our party of seniors stumbled through
one quick verse of song then dispersed laughing, exhausted,
into the chilly night.

As we walked in the door, Robert called and we talked for
an hour or more. I find the phone to be so intimate, mouth to
ear, and we were now in the habit of long phone conversations
which, besides the Internet messages, the odd clipped newspaper article or cartoon sent without notice, kept my feeling
of missing him at a minimum. He was anxious to hear on
several projects, which would take him to the next rung in his
career and he was feeling stressed. I e-mailed him the poem
Ithaca by Constantine Cavafy, which cautions the reader not
to be in a hurry to get to Ithaca. It's the journey that's the reward. Ithaca only supplies the destination, which may or may
not give you the riches you anticipate. He appreciated that.
It said what he needed to hear, and I was grateful to still be
there for him.

For Skiathans, New Year's Day is a special holy day. The
common belief is that whatever a person does on this day he
will do every day throughout the year, so everyone is especially
generous with themselves and to others, a thought I held in
mind as we parked our jeep and walked from the port to one of
Loula's other houses, this one on a narrow cobblestone street in
the village, carrying presents for the family and a crème brulée
for twenty-five people. Anthea, having decided she had been
humiliated enough by not daring to bring anything baked
through the door, decided to make a crème brulée for the Saint
Basil's Day dinner which, because it was not Greek, would not
duplicate anyone else's dessert and would place her immediately in the same culinary class as the other women.

Besides her apartment at Achladies, Loula had two houses in
the village, one in which she sometimes stayed, and one which
she rented. In Skiathos, it was not unusual for a family to have
several houses in the village and several pieces of land on the

mountain, some with *kalivis*, that had been handed down for generations. Extended families tended to live under the same roof, while land was regarded as precious and rarely left idle. Most Skiathans loved nothing more than retreating to their *kalivis* where they could enjoy the quiet, have a family picnic, or clean their olive trees, and many had sheep, goats and chickens, and almost everyone had a garden and, of course, everyone's garden was the best garden, and everyone's olives, wine, and so on. Ooh's and aah's as Mercini took the crème brulée from me, and I thought Anthea was standing a little taller as we melted into the bosom of the family. Loula's food was exquisite and once again I found myself overeating and drinking too much excellent wine, which Spiros poured constantly.

Loula baked the traditional Vasilopitta, pound cake, in which is placed a gold coin. Whoever gets the piece with the coin is said to be blessed and have good luck during the year. Now named in honor of Saint Basil, it also originated with poor, cast aside St. Nicholas, who hid jewels in little cakes that his servants passed out among the poor. Loula cut the cake into twenty pieces and passed them around, allowing the children to pick their pieces first. Everyone slowly chewed their piece of pound cake looking at each other, hoping their next bite would make the New Year special. Slowly, bite by bite the tension mounted, until nearly all of the cake had been eaten and everyone was chewing ever slower, certain the next bite would tell, and someone even asked Loula if she had forgotten to put the coin in. By now, everyone had gathered around the main dining table, when I happened to look over at Loula the moment she bit into the coin and her eyes widened and her mouth dropped and I suddenly saw her at age six as she turned red. Hers was the last piece, rejected by everyone. She wasn't supposed to get the coin. If she could only give it to one of the children. I was happy for her, but I was really more disappointed for myself.

More desserts followed of which the crème brulée seemed the favorite. Everyone especially liked the burnt sugar glaze, a smashing success.

The day after New Year's, Spiros picked me up to take a walk along the river below our house, where Loula wanted to pick wild greens. Nearly seventy, in a grey wool dress below the knee with grey wool stockings and black shoes with a one inch heel, Loula, having never before been on the path, negotiated the sometimes rugged river crossings like a cat, knowing exactly where to step, always elegantly. Then, with her knees bent nearly to the ground and a small kitchen knife, she cut the roots of greens and dropped them in a big clear plastic bag, showing which you could eat, wild spinach here, wild arugula there. After a while, I learned what to look for and Spiros lent me a knife and I helped fill the big bag, harvesting food from the wild earth, which had suddenly become a garden. The dirt was black by the river and we ate plums that had dried out on the trees and were now small sweet prunes. Spiros pointed out a number of olive trees that had become wild from neglect, and the ruins of *kalivis* on land, where older generations planted their gardens because of the river and the black earth, and he mused about buying some of this wild land and housing his animals and building a *kalivi* for himself, so he could sit and listen to the babbling sound of the water, the quiet of the sky.

On January 6th, the ancient Greeks celebrated the birthday of Chronus, the God of Time, a perfect day for Emperor Constantine in his quest for a smooth transition to celebrate the baptism of Christ in the River Jordan, which he named the Feast of the Epiphany, moving Christ's birthday, which was also celebrated on that day, to December 25th, to replace Mithra. According to the Bible, the Epiphany was the day when Mary asked the evangelist John to baptize her son, Jesus, and while he was doing so the Lord made himself manifest through a great light, hence epiphany, and told the gathering the boy was His only son.

The day is a holiday in Greece, and this year it was cold but clear after two days of torrential rain. The grass on the green by the quay was still damp as Anthea and I walked among hundreds of others, moving towards the edge of the port where it intersected the dock. In the water, three fishing boats bobbed about thirty yards away, one filled with young men, two with lifesaving equipment. Everyone, including the Skiathos Philharmonic Band, was waiting for Papa Yiorgos to finish "The Blessing of the Waters" in the cathedral, and then lead a procession down the stone steps to the dock, where a small riser with a microphone was set up. We had stopped to wish *"Chronia pola"* to Tassos, who owned a small grocery store on the corner next to Spiros' store, when the church bells rang and the band began playing and the procession came down the steps to the port, led by the priests and their attendants, who were carrying a large silver caldron of water which had just been blessed. The people crowded along the dock and port, as the young boys on the boat stripped down to tee shirts and bathing suits. The attendants set the caldron on the stage and Papa Yiorgos, with his long white beard, stepped up and continued prayers and incantations, and the children chanted:

"Today is the day!"

Papa Yiorgos continued on and on, until someone from one of the boats yelled:

"Faster, Papa, the boys are getting cold!"

But Papa Yiorgos continued at the same pace, incense, blessings, chants, incense, blessing, chants, and one boy took off his shirt and, waving it, yelled:

"Throw it this way, Papa!"

The chants and prayers continued for what seemed like another ten minutes, as Papa Yiorgos went through the entire

Baptism ritual as if it were any child, and then raised the cross high in the air when the crowd began yelling for its favorite son:

"Yiannis!"

"Panayiotis!"

Then, the church bells rang again and the drums rolled and Papa Yiorgos flung the cross into the water and twenty boys dove into a very cold sea on this very cold day, and for a moment it looked like someone had thrown meat to a school of sharks there was so much thrashing and white water. After a moment, a head popped up, then another, then they went back down again and a few more popped up and disappeared, when suddenly the cross rose out of the water in the hand of Dimitris, the son of a fisherman, amid much applause. Then, the faithful lined up in front of the cauldron, where Papa Nikolas filled their bottles and jars with the water his father had just blessed in the cathedral, which they would save and drink sparingly over the year to restore health. For the rest of the day, Dimitris would carry the cross through the village, being welcomed into the houses as a blessing for the home and for which he would receive coins, some of which he would share with the church.

This day would end the Christmas season. Throughout the next morning, the lights and decorations would be taken down. There was already a noticeable difference in the amount of daylight, every day a little more. The festival had done its work. Spiros and Matoula had invited us for Epiphany dinner at their home at Achladies Beach, sea bass done outside on the barbeque, octopus grilled indoors in the fireplace, and the wild greens we had picked earlier in the week boiled and served with lemon and oil. As I sat by the fire and watched Matoula baste the octopus, Danae, who was now speaking in full sentences, was talking on her toy cell phone to Anthea who was talking back into a TV remote. In this modern age, when new ways were threatening the old, the past weeks had made me realize how wise and important it was that so many people on this island still remained faithful to the old traditions: the discipline of the forty day fast, the season lasting over a month with a series of smaller celebrations, their roots in ancient customs and rituals more spiritual than material, more philosophical and educational than entertaining, although entertaining. For me, it was the most peaceful holiday season I'd ever known, more joyous, more satisfying, so little attention to gift giving, so much to tradition and reaffirmation, which, as Spiros reminded me, was sharing what your ancestors shared with their ancestors for centuries.

WONDERLAND

Numberless are the world's wonders,
but none more wonderful than man.

Sophocles

As February approached, it became colder and I had to turn on the central heating the entire day when it rained, but only in the morning and evening on days when the sun appeared amid small puffy white clouds. I was delighted our new trees were getting a good soaking and our ground water was being replenished. On the weather channel, I started tracking a fierce arctic storm with record low temperatures that was moving slowly down from Russia east and south, the weather map looking increasingly ominous for the poor people in its wake, as the white arctic front moved steadily downwards through the Ukraine, Romania, Bulgaria, across Western Turkey. The following Sunday, in Tassos' small market, I ran into another Tassos, a fifty-year-old red-bearded cherub with a beatific face. Like many Skiathans, he found goods or services lacking on the island, and ways to fill those needs and support himself and his six children. He owned a small shop in the village, which sold diving equipment and also religious icons, and another shop in another part of the village, which was a pet store, while he himself worked for the city, collecting money for fines. Arms filled with groceries, he greeted me warmly as usual and told me he was stocking up on basics:

bread and milk, cheeses and canned goods, because he had a cousin that worked for Olympic Airways who received their weather information from the Greek Air Force who said the Sporades were right in the middle of the path of that arctic storm with huge winds expected, icy temperatures, and a mountain of snow, and it would last three days and begin at three o'clock on Monday in the morning. When I returned home, Anthea said Spiros called to say a terrible storm was coming and that he had put Kostas, the backhoe operator, on notice to keep our road passable, and that if we needed something, to call him. As she was telling me, I noticed out the window that Spiros' pickup was backing up my driveway with its bed piled with chunks of olive wood, cut from pruning his trees. Everyone seemed so hysterical, so unused to a little snow, I had to laugh - I was a Vermonter who as a kid had to exit our house from the second story window at least once or twice every winter.

In the late afternoon, the wind picked up, but by watching the clouds the past few days I had surmised that the storm was moving more west than south, and in fact might even pass us altogether. On Sunday evening, it started to drizzle but it didn't get colder. I went to bed late, waiting for the weather to change, but with the exception of a few fairly strong gusts of wind there was no change. Setting my alarm for 2:45 a.m. to test the accuracy of the Greek Air Force, I awoke and went to my window and saw little difference, although the gusts seemed to have increased in number. After a half hour, I was convinced we were on the very outside of the storm which at that moment was roaring by north of us and we were free, so I went back to my bed. In the morning, the weather hadn't changed and I made a joke at breakfast to Anthea about the Greek Air Force, although lately nothing seemed funny to my bride where Greece or Greeks were concerned, so I laughed to

myself all morning as I went about my life. After a leisurely
Monday lunch, I was standing at the sink, washing the dishes
when, as if someone had thrown a huge blanket over the house,
it suddenly became quite dark and the wind began to howl
and I looked out the window at thick flurries of snow moving
sideways with the largest flakes I'd ever seen. I looked at the
clock on the wall, 3:04. At first, I thought Tassos must have
confused morning for afternoon, then I remembered Greeks
don't consider afternoon until after their long lunch and nap,
so for Tassos 3:00 in the morning was my 3:00 in the afternoon
and the Greek Air Force was right. All of a sudden, the wind
sounded like it would burst through the windows and I hadn't
shuttered any and I couldn't conceive of trying at that moment, so I waited, poised between gusts, and finally battened
down everything. Then, I ran to the woodpile and carried a few
stacks to the side of the fireplace in the living room, when the
lights flickered and I instantly realized what losing electricity
would mean, since everything we depended upon depended
upon it, water, heat, lights. I immediately started a fire using
several pinecones. The fire was soon roaring and I felt a sweet
thrill in having started it so quickly. I went to the television,
newly confident I was in charge and started looking for the
weather channel when the lights went out.

Anthea immediately started prepping dinner early, taking
advantage of the dark grey daylight, while for the next two
hours, the lights would come on for a second or two, creating
an expectation that in a minute they would be more permanent; but they weren't, and as darkness descended upon us, we
lit candles and armed ourselves with flashlights. Spiros called:

"Are you okay? Do you have a generator?"

"A generator? You think we need a generator?"

"Yes. Always."

"Well, don't worry, we're fine. We have the oven on and a
good fire and the house is comfortable enough and we're going

to bed early anyway and by tomorrow we'll have electricity. But thank you, it's so sweet of you to be concerned."

The warmest place was in bed under our comforter, which was where we were by 7:30, although I was awake most of the night, waiting for the house to fall down from the wind. The next morning, at first light, the windows were completely covered in ice and snow. We were still without electricity, so I jumped out of bed and into my clothes, turned the oven on high again, and had a roaring fire before Anthea came down layered in sweaters, a coat and scarf, hat and gloves. The countryside was a winter wonderland and we were astonished at the amount of snow that had accumulated in such a short time. Still falling sideways, thick as lace, swirling in the roaring wind, it reminded me of winter in Vermont and it seemed oddly comforting. Breakfast was fun. We were out of our normal routine, having another adventure. Tasoula called:

"Are you okay? Don't you have a generator?"

She said I should check the road and if I think I can't get out, she would call the mayor and get it plowed. Positive I could get out with my jeep and its oversized tires and 2-gear 4-wheel drive, I brushed a foot and a half of snow off my hood and windshield, climbed in, turned the key, heard ga ah ah, then nothing. Suddenly slightly alarmed, I hurried knee deep in snow back into the house on the phone to Tasoula. She would make some calls and find someone to come out right away. Hanging up, I realized the fire was dying and I was out of wood, so I kicked off my boots and hurried to stir the fire which, when you have other things to do, takes a lot of tending to keep alive. It made me wonder how before electricity they managed to get anything else done as I piled snow covered wood beside the fireplace, then under the kitchen table, dry wood now being out of the question, and each time I walked out into the storm, I was reminded of W.C. Fields in *The Fatal Glass of Beer*:

"T'aint a fit night out for man nor beast!"

Only it was the middle of the day. But it was still fun, although I could see how two more days of this might become tiresome.

In a few minutes, Tasoula and Stamatis plowed their way up the driveway in an SUV with chains. Everyone else was evidently booked. Afraid the fierce wind would tear off the hoods of the two vehicles as we opened them, I held mine and Tasoula held theirs, while Stamatis attached the cables and we waited for a lull. At that moment, Tasoula held both hoods while I jumped in the car and in a few seconds the engine came to life. Tasoula advised me to keep the jeep running for a few minutes but not to try to go down the mountain without chains.

"I have chains!" I vigorously pronounced, pulling the chains out of the back, "I bought them at the supermarket!"

Tasoula and Stamatis gave each other a look, then immediately went down on their knees and, with bare hands in the blinding blizzard, tried to put chains on one of my tires. After about five minutes and much trying and some analysis, they decided the chains were probably too small for my oversized tires. We adjourned for coffee in the living room, which seemed to be slowly growing colder since the day before, in spite of the fire, and we remained in our coats. Stamatis said the temperature in our house was the same as theirs even with central heat, because their house had stone floors, which were always cold. After coffee, they decided to try the chains again and both crawled on their backs under the jeep in the snow. I couldn't believe it. And I couldn't say how many people on earth I would have done that for but, and it's probably to my shame, there aren't very many. Perhaps even none. After they left, Spiros called to say Yiannis was coming up in the truck to feed the animals and that we should come back with him and stay with them at their house in Achladies. I told him we were still okay but if the electricity wasn't back on by 3:00 in the afternoon, we'd come; but if Yiannis was coming up, could he bring us some water as our pump wasn't working.

"Ten minutes", he said and held his hand over the phone as he gave Yiannis the order for water, "He brings you bread, too. Anything else? Any time you want to come, don't worry about snow, Kostas will come with the tractor to bring you here."

After I hung up, the phone rang again, it was another Kostas, Papa Yiorgos' son-in-law:

"Are you okay? Do you have a generator?"

By 3:00 that afternoon, even with a roaring fire the house was getting too cold to be bearable and I was just about to call Spiros when the phone rang. It was Matoula.

"Do you have electricity?"

"No", I replied with a slight whine, "And we'd like to come and stay with you."

"Bravo! I will tell Spiros."

Anthea was napping as I strode into the bedroom.

"Get up, pal, we gotta get outa here. Spiros is sending his jeep."

She bolted up and looked at me just as the lights went on. "What???"

"Nothing, honey, go back to sleep."

After twenty hours, the lights were suddenly back on. In a minute, Anthea was yawning at the counter in the kitchen, prepping for dinner, pre-cooking potatoes and carrots for the roast leg of lamb when the flame under the pan went out.

"We're out of gas. Change to the other can."

I took a breath, "We've already used it."

"We have no gas?"

"We've been heating the house with the oven all this time."

"I give up."

"I'll call Spiros."

Five minutes later, Spiros' friend, Yiannis, a large sandy haired walrus with a huge appetite for life, knocked on the kitchen window with a grin and took us to Achladies where we were greeted by Spiros and Matoula, and seven of their friends, five of whom were on cell phones, who it seemed always dropped by, especially during a storm. Together with Mercini, Danae, and Loula, we were twelve for dinner, roasted pork from Spiros' pig, which Anthea and Matoula cooked, and for dessert Loula made little donuts, and it happened to be the eve of Matoula's birthday and everyone sang the traditional Greek birthday song, wishing beautiful Matoula health and long life, and much wine was being drunk.

Anthea took me aside, "Where are we sleeping?"

"In the bedroom over there, where we put our stuff."

"Where are they sleeping?"

"Where?"

"Yes. I don't see a second bedroom. I only see this."

She showed me a room that was used as an office with a desk, a chair and a simple set of bunk beds. We felt terrible, we didn't know what to do; we couldn't go home, not to mention didn't want to go home. There was only one small hotel in the village still open, but it was probably impossible to get there by now and was most likely full. We had a hurried conference with Spiros and Matoula, who insisted they sleep in that room whenever they have company, and they would be hurt if we decided not to stay. Wasn't their bedroom comfortable enough for us?

Considering the events of the last day and a half, it was no surprise that we both slept like logs. I awoke first early Wednesday morning and went into the living room and sat by the fireplace near a heater. The blizzard was still raging and the snow covering the roofs was several feet deep. Icicles as big as swords hung from the eaves. A calico cat outside the window sat on the marble ledge, huddled on a piece of cloth just large enough for his four paws and tail bone. A group of crows sat on the leeward side of a huge eucalyptus tree, huddled against the wind.

The cat closed his eyes, trying to sleep sitting up. Then two cell phones began ringing, then the land line, and the house was up. Matoula was making espressos and toast, and Spiros was organizing an expedition with Yiannis to take his men up to his land to feed the animals and take me home to turn on a water faucet to a trickle to keep the pipes from freezing, leave food for Pappou, shake the snow off the citrus trees and cypresses that were in danger of breaking, and check up on things at the house in general.

Yiannis barreled Spiros' jeep with chains on four tires up our unplowed road, slipping and sliding and making me very nervous because on my side we were only several yards from a two hundred foot drop and I was having a very hard time finding the lock for the seat belt I was suddenly trying to fasten. And Yiannis was plowing until too much snow had piled up in front of him and he would back up ten feet and blast ahead another twenty feet, back up ten, blast twenty, until finally we were past the drop-off, but the snow was well over the hood and the tires were deep into the mud and the jeep was stuck fast.

I never made it to the house. Spiros' men climbed through the waist deep snow the last seventy-five yards to the barn, fed the animals, then came back with a shovel and a baby lamb, six days old, the smallest of a pair born to a ewe with only one working teat. She had been pushed aside by her larger sibling and hadn't eaten and was so weak she couldn't stand up. The boys only first noticed, because they hadn't been able to be there to tend to them these past few days. And now they were taking the baby home to bottle feed her and pray they were in time. After laying her on the back seat, the boys dug and with a great deal of effort we all pushed and rocked until we unstuck the jeep and backed out to the larger road, causing me once again to have great anxiety as we sped past the drop-off in reverse. On the way home, we were stopped by Dimitris, the new vice mayor, who explained he had my road plowed twice yesterday and they were coming up again within the hour.

We had a beautiful lunch at Loula's, pasta and breaded pork cutlets from the pig that kept on giving, then a nap, then coffee and apple cake, then wine and then another wonderful dinner for eight at Spiros' and Matoula's. We were suddenly on some wonderful vacation, sharing a house with good friends, only we were taking their bedroom, so on the next morning, after coffee, I insisted Anthea and I go home. After trying to dissuade us, Spiros finally called Kostas and his plow to lead us. I realized then even though he always says, "Call me if you need something" I never have to. He anticipates the thing before I even know I need it. With Kostas' help we made it home where the electricity was running and our house was toasty warm. I spent the first few hours hosing the snow off the citrus as Spiros had suggested. Having felt guilty abandoning our home, it was comforting to be back, catching the news on the weather channel. Our adventure had been a wonderful break and much fun, but it would also be nice to slip back into our winter rhythm.

That night, the baby lamb drank a third of a bottle of milk, then went to sleep and never woke up. I had taken for granted the sweet little creature would have a happy ending.

In a few days the roads would be clear, the sun would warm a cloudless sky and I would walk through the melting snowscape in a sweatshirt, sneakers, and sunglasses. Sometimes I would take a new route, a distance of about three miles, which would begin off the main road and wind up a narrow country lane, through a pine forest along a high ridge of a finger of land known as the Kalamaki Peninsula, which had glorious views that extended from the mainland to Euboea, to Skopelos, and to Skiathos village. Then I would power walk my way back down the mountain to the main road and to my starting point - an aerobic workout.

It was during these walks that I began talking to myself.

Sometimes laughing loudly, even crying. It became therapy. I would relive old conversations where I had been humiliated and tongue-tied and prepare myself, should the same moment recur, with the perfect response. There was nothing like saying it out loud I discovered. What seemed smart to me, when spoken, sometimes sounded quite stupid. I also discovered that, as an injustice collector, when my mind was set free, invariably the memory of some slight, real or imagined, would rise to the surface. I vowed to examine that. The forest and the sea had become my analyst's office, and since no one was around I could continue the long look back at my life with a new freedom.

With each passing day I was falling more and more in love with my new world, while the old was receding further into the shadows, as if I had gone from childhood to childhood with no time in between. Other than loved ones, there was nothing we missed, maybe a sports car on a well-paved mountain road twice a week, but the roads on Skiathos were challenging even with a jeep, so I wasn't especially hungry for man over machine. Anthea only missed sweet midget gherkins. We would laugh, it was such a small price to pay, then spit three times all over the place.

It was almost painful not being able to speak the language well enough to convey to the Skiathans my appreciation of their society, truly the most evolved I'd ever known, and my gratitude at being allowed to be a part of it. For the rest of the winter, the island would remain ours, we who endured it, all stepping together. It was a wonderful time of year, and it seemed to pass so quickly.

TO THE HOLY MOUNTAIN

What is God? Everything.

Pindar

According to early Byzantine religious writings, when the Apostles drew straws to divide up the areas where they would preach, the Virgin Mary wanted to be included. Her straw indicated Asia Minor but, on the journey to Cyprus, the ship encountered a terrible storm which threw it off course, forcing the captain to put in at Macedonia, where the Angel Gabriel appeared to the Virgin and pointed to Mount Athos, a green mountain peninsula of some 130 square miles, and told her it was there that she should begin her ministry. It was also written that when she reached the peninsula, she heard a voice:

"From now on, this shall be your estate and your garden and paradise, as well as a haven of salvation for those who wish to be saved, and a recourse and a refuge and a calm harbor of repentance for those burdened with many sins."

The first monk appeared on the mountain in the 7th century. By the 10th, a self governing republic of monasteries of various foundations and nationalities had evolved, all dedicated to the Virgin, which obeyed with varying strictness the rules St. Basil had drawn up in the 4th century enjoining study and labor. In the 11th century, having discovered that the wives and daughters of shepherds who came to the mountain to sell milk and wool were too great a temptation for the monks, the

Byzantine emperor, Constantine Monomachus, issued a decree that women would no longer be admitted to this mountain dedicated to a woman. By the end of the 11th century, nothing feminine, not even a cat or a hen was allowed, and now over a thousand years later, other than the relaxation of the cat rule, there are still none but working animals on the mountain, male dogs and donkeys. Nothing female is allowed even close to the shore, which is patrolled and enforced by the Greek Coast Guard with prison sentences from two to twelve months for violators.

Although Mount Athos lies within Greece, it is a self-governing republic which falls within the purview of the Ministry of Foreign Affairs. Like the Vatican to Italy, Mt. Athos is ruled solely by the heads of twenty working monastic establishments which exist in various forms and sizes around the peninsula in different categories: from huge monasteries to hermitages, the harshest form of Orthodox monastic life, with some monks living in caves in the vertical side of Athos, virtually inaccessible by land, their only access to the sea by a series of pulleys and ropes.

Spiros had been to the Holy Mountain every year since his teens. Long walks through the forests and along the cliffs from monastery to monastery, quiet time for contemplation, the simple beauty of the services and the Spartan simplicity of the life appealed to him, and at times he even stayed a month or more and made friends with some of the monks. One evening, during the great winter snow storm, he offered to take me for a few days at which time the girls decided they would go to Thessalonika and do girl things.

Even Greeks needed a visa to enter Mount Athos, and the visa is granted for only the days the pilgrim plans to visit and the monasteries in which he plans to stay. Since the days are dependent on monastery bed availability, even in the middle of winter, we needed to plan a month ahead. To that end, Spiros faxed a copy of my passport to the Holy Board of Overseers with a declaration of my religion, Maronite Catholic and, on a morning in late February, we were sailing under a welcome winter sun to the mainland on a forty-two foot fishing kayiki which Spiros had quickly arranged the night before, because the ferry operators suddenly decided to strike. He was intent on making our dates.

A cold drizzly week had suddenly turned to spring and the sun was reflecting a stream of fire inside the kayiki's wake. I leaned against the railing next to Yiannis, a wiry young fisherman in his twenties, while he squinted up at an approaching cloud and shouted over the engine a simple wisdom it had taken me a lifetime to grasp:

"Not much money, fishing, but good for your soul!" he grinned, "You're free!"

In Volos, Spiros and I followed the girls north for several hours in rental cars, passing Olympus, home of the gods, high above all the other mountains, covered in a smooth white blanket of snow. Then, along the sea, through farmland fed by ancient streams that flowed from Olympus with names like Spring of Artemis, Spring of Aphrodite, of Athena, so many more familiar ancient names, places, and legends. Then a coffee shop stop and almost tearful hugs and goodbyes, although we were only going for two nights. The girls' car turned off for Thessalonika and Spiros and I continued north towards the Holy Mountain. I was looking forward to it.

Once, during my philosophy major days at Xavier, a Jesuit university in Cincinnati, I went to Lexington Kentucky during spring break to visit a Trappist monastery called Gethsemani, where Thomas Merton, the most celebrated Catholic mystic and writer of the time, was in residence. As I knelt in the loft of the candlelit stone chapel, looking down and listening to the monks chant their vespers and wondering which was the revered mystic whose books I had been admiring, a man in the bell tower above began playing a sweet solo trumpet. Completely unanticipated by me, it deeply moved me by its simple beauty, a taste of what Mr. Merton might have called spiritual ecstasy. Trappists aren't allowed to speak or have visitors. They work seven days a week and are never allowed to leave the grounds. And yet, on that night in that chapel, overwhelmed by that transcendent moment, being a Trappist seemed quite appealing.

Riding with Spiro in a somber silence, I began thinking about our privileged, almost painfully beautiful life. I was reminded of the morning I was sitting in Dimitra's taverna by myself, having a coffee and reading the paper, when an old Englishman paused and asked me if it was our house that had just been built and that he could see from the valley, to which I proudly answered that it was and it was my wife Anthea's design.

"It happens to everybody" he said, leaning on his cane, "You build your dream house then in a couple of years one or the other dies."

Then he shook his head as if brushing off an ugly memory and walked away.

I never saw the old man again but he lived forever in my head. Our whole life was each other. It had been carved into the hillside together. Anthea couldn't possibly live there by herself. She simply wasn't physically capable. I had no idea what I would do, whether I would go somewhere else or stay and live alone on the island. And where would we be buried?

On Skiathos, the dead are laid out at home in their living room in the morning, where friends and family come by and sit with the bereaved, eating sweets and sipping coffee and liqueur until the afternoon, when they carry the open coffin through the village, followed by Jimmie carrying the lid. The procession proceeds to the cathedral, where there is a service by Papa Yiorgos, after which Jimmie puts the lid on the coffin and

the deceased is carried up the hill to the small cemetery, a pine
and cypress forest on a seaside cliff with a breathtaking view of
the Aegean. The body lies in that idyllic scene for three years,
when the bones are disinterred and then washed and stored in
a small private ossuary on ancestral property.

The graves themselves are intimate and personal with pictures and relics of the deceased. The coffin is actually above
ground, planted in a bed of rich dirt where loved ones usually make a flower garden. On favorable nights, women sit on
benches at the entrance to the small memorial park and gossip.

Down the street from my mother's house in a well-groomed
suburb of Hartford Connecticut, inside a tall, strong, acres-
long wrought iron fence was the Fairview Cemetery, where my
father was buried at age fifty-five. On one of the broad front
gates there was a large dark green metal sign with gold letters
which read:

> NO artificial flowers allowed between May 15 and No-
>   vember 1
> Only clay pots under 10 inches and baskets under 12
>   inches allowed – all other containers will be removed
> Only one pot or basket allowed per grave
> Pots are NOT allowed to be dug into the soil
> NO dogs allowed in the cemetery
> Flags and flag holders will be permitted from the third
>   Saturday in May to the first Saturday in June and
>   from the first Saturday in November until the third
>   Saturday in November – flags and flag holders left
>   after these dates shall be removed
> NO parking on grass

"Where would you rather go?"

Anthea and I joked about it occasionally, and then sometimes quite seriously. We both liked the cemetery in Skiathos. The idea that one could have a flower garden where the other lay buried, and could sit and look out at the sea through the pines might even help ease the unbearable loss, and then in three years, to be washed and placed in a small stone ossuary shaped like a Byzantine church in a nice aspect near our house. There was no funeral home on Skiathos, no morgue, no place to store a body, so the burial usually took place within hours of the death. There would be no time for friends or relatives to arrive from America. And yet, being carried through the village in a suit that, because I had eaten so much since my arrival, was much too small for me but had been slit in the back so in death it looked just perfect, Jimmie walking with the lid, friends and neighbors in the procession, people who had become part of my new life, Papa Yiorgos blessing me on my journey, and then resting in a charming cemetery by the sea with the sound of women chatting on the benches, it all sounded quite charming.

One night, we came to the conclusion that if anything happened to me, Anthea should go to Athens and get a chic apartment and another black standard poodle like Guido and maybe even design an opera or a play. She had friends there and would live the life she once suspected she might: a little old white haired widow in black, living in a great building with a great dog. It had never occurred to me that it wouldn't be me who would go first. I was the man. Women supposedly lived five and a half years longer. But now, having not been away from Anthea for more than two hours in the last few years, I began wondering what if I actually outlived Anthea and my life was to be in five rather than three acts, Elizabethan rather than Greek drama, and having been given the gods' glimpse of happiness in the third, I would be brought low in the fourth, a widower, broke and bereft, alone and utterly reduced at the end of act five?

I was sinking into a small depression as we passed the ruins
of Stagirus, Aristotle's birth place, and continued along a high
coastal road with sheer cliffs that reminded me of California's
Big Sur, through a pine forest where, at every clearing across
the bay above a range of green mountains, I could now see
the daunting and forbidding awesome white pyramid peak of
Athos, the Holy Mountain. Then, we crossed Xerxes Canal,
dug by his army for his navy to pass through on their way to
their first battle with the Greeks in front of my house. It was
dusk when we entered the small port village of Ouranoupolis,
City of Heaven, where our visas were waiting and where we
would take the boat in the morning down the peninsula to
Athos.

Ouranoupolis appeared dark and mysterious as we strolled
down the center of the deserted main street and as we entered
a small empty neon lit taverna, where we interrupted an old
bald waiter drinking beer and reading a newspaper and ordered
fish and wine as we sat down. Six old and weathered fishermen
shuffled through the door.

"Do you have meat? We only want meat!"

Two of them were captains. That day, both had dropped
nets as deep as a thousand feet and came up nearly empty and,
as they sat down, they complained that it was because the wind
was coming from Africa. After a moment, an old woman entered and went into the kitchen and a loud argument ensued
between the woman and the waiter because he was drunk again.
Then the waiter appeared by his station with a smirk and tried
to pour wine from a jug into a half-liter copper pitcher, spill-
ing it on everything including himself, and the men laughed
and drank and the waiter went back into the kitchen where
the woman began yelling again. But the fish was excellent and
the fishermen ate their souvlaki with gusto. We all laughed at
the waiter as he laughed at himself, trying once again not to
spill wine as he poured from the jug to the pitcher. Late that

night, in the shadow of a streetlight, in a small room overlooking an alley between two streets, I lay awake troubled by the
thought of my life in five acts, complete with scenarios, most of
them horrifying, like replacing the waiter in that taverna, living
alone and friendless at Ouranoupolis, City of Heaven, drinking too much beer, and always dying on the toilet, and it wasn't
until dawn that I sank into a welcome deep sleep.

The next morning, it was cloudy and cold when we boarded
a boat that looked like a city bus. With a number of other men,
including three monks in black habits with long beards, we
took a silent forty-minute ride in rough water, in which two of
the pilgrims became sick. Like a bus, the boat stopped quickly
along the peninsula at different piers, where out of the mist 9th
and 10th century Athonite monasteries appeared, huge com-
plexes of buildings, great ash colored fortresses the size of small
medieval villages, with timber balconies under domed cupo-
las and massive buttresses, awesome, regal, inspiring. Passing a
small herd of wild horses grazing in a chestnut forest, we finally
landed at our stop, the main port of Athos, which consisted of
a small concrete pier with a custom's office, two souvenir shops
and a closed café.

No one spoke as we boarded a van filled with assorted pilgrims. We were hauled over cobblestones, then a dirt and mud
road, passing a number of small *kalivis* in the hills en route to
Karyes, the capital of the small republic. Besides the one 18th
century building, where government business was conducted,
the sum of the capital was a 13th century church which was being held up by steel girders, two closed souvenir shops, a general store, and a nearly empty café. The sun never appeared, and
it was cold inside the church as we visited the heralded 14th
and 16th century frescoes lighted only by a few dark stained
glass windows and several votive candles.

Leaving the church, it began raining softly. We passed down
stone steps that became narrower as they continued out of the

capitol, until they became a thousand year old foot-polished cobble stone path down the mountain, which wound through a pine forest along a quiet stream. The rain soon stopped but the day stayed overcast and cold. Spiros fashioned me a walking stick from a branch of chestnut that came in very handy on the slippery stones. We continued until early afternoon, when we were met on the road by a very thin young monk, barely twenty, Aristides, a Fayum painting with a thin patch of black chin hair on an otherwise hairless boy's face. He was huddled inside a shabby black wool habit with rips and tears, under an oversize black sweater with holes at the elbows, black torn sneakers and a black watch cap. He spoke a few words to Spiros, then disappeared back into the forest and we continued on a narrow dirt road until we approached a *kalivi* with a small chapel and a workshop for making incense. Aristides greeted us again and led us into the *kalivi*.

Standing at a pot belly stove in a similarly tattered robe, a cast iron pan in his hand turning over potatoes in olive oil, Spiros' friend, Nikitas, a strong, square monk in his late thirties with a big black beard, smiled broadly as we entered and insisted we sit and have lunch and wouldn't hear that we didn't have time. After we all clinked glasses of thin red wine with the monks' customary toast, *"Kalo Parathiso"*, good paradise, Spiros and Nikitas sat back and talked in Greek, while I ate the potatoes and mushrooms, avocado slices with oranges, olives, feta cheese, garlic cloves eaten like cashews, and hot peppers. I was starved and everything tasted so fresh and clean. The wine made me light headed, and as cookies and candies and Greek coffee were served, I looked around the small spare room with the one long table and two benches, a small sink and cupboard, a few icons, and it felt quite cozy. Then the sky darkened and it started to drizzle and I looked around for a light and realized there was none. No electricity. No generator. No light. No refrigerator. No heat other than the pot belly stove in this uncluttered house the size of a Hollywood dressing room trailer. This was their life and, although Spiros and I were buttoned up in our coats, the monks weren't the least bit cold in their threadbare habits, laughing and talking, clear eyed, energetic and cheerful while I sat on my hands, too embarrassed to put on my gloves.

Another hour along the stone road, then a detour through the woods and we stopped at another small *kalivi* where outside on a tree stump sat a small white cardboard box of loukoums, sugared jelly, and spring water for the pilgrim. Spiros had become friends with an old monk revered for his wisdom that had resided here but had passed away during the year, and he wanted to light a candle for his friend in the small chapel. After a loukoum and a can of water, I was feeling energetic and we continued through the forest for another hour, until we stopped at the crest of a hill and looked down on a large olive grove, down to the sea surrounding what looked like a medieval town. In fact, it was the breathtaking 10th century Monastery of Iveron, our home for the night.

It was cold and damp and quickly becoming dark in the grey stone courtyard. There were no lights and no one around when Spiros led me into one of the three large chapels, where the monks were in the middle of vespers. It was warmer inside the vestibule but very dark, lighted only by one candle. I could barely make out the frescoes, which covered every inch of wall. Brimming with anticipation, I tiptoed into the main part of the chapel, lighted by only two candles and where the smell of incense was almost overwhelming. In Gethsemani, I was only allowed to observe from a loft. I had never been so close to so many monks in the middle of their service, hooded men with long beards in black robes inches away from me, holy men. I stood transfixed while an ordained monk performed a ritual unchanged since the 9th century in a low mesmerizing voice.

Vespers began every day two hours before sunset and finished fifteen minutes before sunset, so even before my eyes had completely adjusted to the darkness, the monks and the twenty or so pilgrims lined up and took a small piece of bread, which the priest held in a basket, then kissed his hand and left the chapel. I followed Spiros outside and was soon shivering in the damp cold when the doors to the dining hall opened and we silently followed forty or more monks into a long narrow un-heated room, where they quietly stood at one long cold marble table and we at another, until the abbot said grace, whereupon everyone sat and wasted no time eating. In exactly fifteen min-utes, the abbot slapped the table and we all rose for the prayer to thank God for that brief but excellent repast, four small grilled fish, coleslaw, bread, feta, a small glass of thin red wine, and an orange, eaten quickly but silently while a monk at a lectern read a story about the yearning for beauty, written by a monk in the 11th century. For the monks, food was for suste-nance only, not for bodily pleasure. It was also rare to have fish, Spiros told me later; it must have been a celebration.

In the courtyard, afterwards, several monks paused to speak to a few pilgrims and I realized, unlike Nikitas, these were well-heeled monks with handsome wool habits and spotless black down winter coats. Before we could approach any, the court-yard quickly emptied, with the monks going one way and the pilgrims retiring to their rooms, leaving Spiros and me. We still hadn't checked in and, as dim lights appeared in the rooms and passageways, Spiros led me to a dark building whose reception area was lighted by a single bulb where we were greeted hastily by a monk who seemed annoyed to be taking charge, because the monk whose job it ordinarily was had suddenly become ill. "I hope it wasn't the fish", I said quietly, hoping to make him smile, but he looked at me humorlessly as Spiros handed him our visas and he handed him our cell key. On the way to our cell, we strolled around the courtyard of the monastery, established and continually functioning for over a thousand years. Now inhabited by a community of forty-five monks, it employed a small Albanian crew to do the heavier lifting and stoking. Impeccably maintained, it had been well endowed with priceless treasures, both religious and secular, with coins and relics, medieval garments and illuminated manuscripts, to the first printing press copy ever of Homer's Iliad from 1488. After passing the incongruity of a monk in his ancient habit, speaking into a cell phone, we decided it was too cold, wet and dark for another turn and we climbed the stairs to the fourth floor of our dormitory, passing the communal toilets, all squatters, to our heated cell, an austere space with white walls and a flagstone floor, a writing desk with an oil lamp and a box of small wooden matches, and iron beds, where we read for a few minutes then soon fell asleep.

Following Saint Basil's rule for the morning service, eight hours after sunset, that morning at 2:30 the chapel warning bell rang and Spiros rose quietly and left. I rolled over. At 4:30, I slipped into the chapel lit by only three candles and stood behind Spiros. As I watched the congregation of monks in their long black robes, their faces hidden under long beards and hoods, bowing deeply and blessing themselves in broad gestures which started at the floor, responding to the prayers of an ordained monk as he swung his censor, and an old monk with a long white beard ceremoniously blew out one candle in one part of the dark chapel and lit one in another, and another, then blew out another, I felt as if I had stepped into some primitive ancient ritual dedicated to a virgin goddess and the monks were her slaves, like ancient priests to the virgin Athena. Yet, this was now and these men had, in fact, given up every worldly pleasure to dedicate their lives to this Virgin and, in the middle of every night at this time, they would be bowing low to instill humility while praying to her, begging for their redemption. The monks quickly returned to their cells while the pilgrims were led into the cold, dimly lit dining hall for a cup of hot wild sage tea with bread and olives, after which we would be free until the 9:00 a.m. lunch. There were no showers, the monks towel bathed and, since the bathrooms were unheated, it was simply too cold to try. So we went back to our rooms and slept in our clothes and read until the bell rang to announce another fifteen minute meal in our coats: warm lentil soup, plain romaine lettuce leaves, bread, water, no wine, ground walnuts, and an apple. We ate vigorously but silently, as the monk standing at the podium continued reading about the yearning for beauty. It was this monastery Nikitas inhabited for ten years but which he left, feeling that it had become too much like a hotel when it began generating electricity for light.

After checking out of our cell with the same hapless monk, we stopped at Iveron's gift shop to have something to take home. I bought a wool bag, good for the beach. While paying for the bag, the monk behind the counter, a tall dark lanky man in his thirties, heard me speaking English and asked me where I was from in the States in a perfect American accent. Younger than most of the monks and more cordial than the others, Leonidas told me he had been a resident of Iveron for six years. He was Greek and, when his parents divorced and his mother married a Greek-American, he and his sister moved with them to Chicago, but he missed Greece and finally returned. He seemed eager to talk and as we chatted I asked him if he had much time for reading. He answered about two hours a day. When I asked him what he was currently reading, he seemed embarrassed, then reached under the counter and produced a child's book on animals with many colored pictures. As an afterthought, he blurted out *O Neos Theologos* ("The New Theologian") by a 9th century monk named Simeon, but I suspected he was reading mostly about animals. When I asked him if he was happy, he looked at me wistfully.

"It's all the same" he said. "Just like you, we have good days and not so good days, happy days and sad ones. We all carry a cross through our life; it just depends on how you choose to carry it."

As we continued on our way down the stone path, his words haunted me. I always thought being a monk was supposed to somehow help ease the burden, yet for him it only shifted it. Spiros offered me some chocolate:

"From Matoula." He broke me off a piece. "I told her I didn't want it but she said it would remind me of her", he grinned. For me Anthea packed long underwear - the difference after thirty years.

We continued through the forest until mid afternoon, when the sun finally began to appear and we arrived at our home for the night, the 10th century Monastery of Stavronika, the smallest and poorest of the twenty, situated on a bluff overlooking the sea. We were warmly welcomed by five young, energetic monks sitting at a table surrounded by benches and an inviting pot belly stove. In their small spare common room, they made us Greek coffee and passed around loukoums, all the while laughing and chatting with Spiros. We were enjoying a camaraderie that didn't seem possible at solemn and unwelcoming Iveron.

Our cell was a Spartan room with wooden beds, a desk, and an oil lamp, where we dropped our backpacks and went to the church for vespers. Sitting in the cold church, watching the same monks, now hooded and mysterious, my mind kept returning to Leonidas isolated from the world in a group that seemed cheerless, giving up so much and receiving so little. He might have been happier here at Stavronika among monks his own age and closer to his temperament but, having never known another monastery, he would remain at Iveron probably for the rest of his life, adrift, a clerk in a gift shop, day after day after day, and he was still a young man.

Cold bean soup, olives, hot peppers, bread, water, and an avocado for our fifteen minute dinner at 6:30 p.m. in the cold dining room, no wine, no oil, no cheese, no one reading, no talking. Back to our cold room for a nap until 2:30 a.m., when morning services started. After reading the monastery rules on a card in our room in English, I realized I was expected to attend all services. So I sat in the cold dark in the middle of the night for four more hours, while a priest read from various texts in two different chapels, watching the monks bowing and crossing themselves. I could only imagine what story each had to tell, what led each to renounce all worldly pleasure for an uninterrupted life of work and prayer. For some, I assumed, it would have been as told to Mary, "a recourse and a refuge and a calm harbor of repentance for those burdened with many sins." For others, no doubt, it must have been to live free from the temptations of the flesh in order to pursue a life of the spirit. As I sat through what seemed like an endless service, I wondered if it ever occurred to them that if they believed God created them, wouldn't He have known what He was doing when He created their duality and that to try to alter the balance, nurturing one nature while trying to deny the other, was an attempt to improve His creation and was nothing less than hubris? I was clearly becoming cranky and, by the fourth hour, I was concentrating more on not falling asleep and out of my chair, when the monks finally lined up for bread and I was suddenly given a second wind.

Tea and bread in the dining hall where you could see your breath, no olives, then the usual nap and read until 9:00 a.m., when the lunch bell rang and we stood at our table, waiting for the abbot to finish grace so we could commence eating, one small fish, another celebration, and a glass of thin red wine. It was impossible not to take pleasure in it. Twenty minutes later, most of the monks would be leaving for the forest in vans, with chainsaws to cut and collect firewood for the furnaces until vespers, but for Spiros and me it would be time to catch the shuttle back to Ouranoupolis.

I was grateful to be leaving, not for the creature comforts, but rather the recognition during the past two days that somewhere along the way, from Gethsemani to Stavronika, I had lost my faith. The notions of The Redeemer, of Heaven and Hell, doctrines I took for granted but perhaps never fully believed and hadn't contemplated in years, now seemed like childish myths and I was convinced would one day be generally viewed like Greek mythology. And yet, being moved by the depth of the monks' innocence and their commitment, so intimate and personal, I was becoming increasingly embarrassed and guilty at being an intruder and was convinced I should never have come. In the days that would follow, I would realize that, besides losing my faith, I must have lost the childlike innocence necessary for that kind of faith, the same kind that allows you to fall in love, and I was saddened by it. And through the next weeks, especially in my walks around Koukounaries, I would try to examine where and when and how far I'd come from Gethsemani, or gone, from the innocence which allowed the monastic life to appeal to me as a student until now.

A monk once told Spiros:

"When you're dancing with another man's wife, you're dancing with the devil."

Just as you can die from a thousand cuts, you can also lose your soul in the thousands of tastes, temptations, addictions, passions, pleasures, which then become necessities until they become the dictates to the soul, much like the inversion of living to work instead of working to live. In the short while I had been in Skiathos, my life was the simplest yet most gratifying I'd ever known, and I wondered if perhaps the monks weren't right, and if as a student I had continued simplifying my life instead of grasping for more, I would through stages have become more like Yiannis the fisherman, wise without much money, but happy, then like Nikitas the monk, without electricity, perhaps even happier, then taking to living in a cave with the only access by pulleys and ropes from the sea, contemplating the Divine, happiest of all. But I would never know. Lost innocence is so hard to recover. Besides, during my time on Athos, I realized with ever-greater clarity how much I enjoyed and was helplessly dependent on the company of women.

On the boat back to Ouranoupolis, Spiros warned me that all women look beautiful when you first leave the mountain. At the port, the first woman I saw was chubby and middle aged, buying fish from the back of a pickup truck, and it was true. I was struck by her natural beauty, and I laughed for five minutes. It was also the first laugh I'd had in two days.

We caught up with the girls, who also looked especially feminine and beautiful, in a restaurant on the quay in Volos. It seemed like two weeks since we left them at the coffee stop and, as they laughingly recalled their adventures in Thessalonika and I sat without my coat at a table set with linen, in an armchair, drinking thick fruity red wine, enjoying a leisurely meal of meat and pasta and a chocolate dessert, I thought of those poor men who, much more important than carnal pleasures, would never enjoy the company of women, a mother, a favorite aunt, sister, daughter, or hear the angelic laugh of a child. And if it was true that we all carried a cross through life and it just depended on how you chose to carry it, if it was all the same to anyone, I preferred to carry mine in Skiathos where, like Pindar, I seemed to find God in everything: the sheep grazing in the valley below our house, the old lady who gave me the icon by the church, a glass of wine, a night sky. I still believed in the Garden of Eden. I just believed I was living in it. And so long as I was a good husband to my wife and to my property, and loved my neighbors, which I did, I believed if there was *Kalo Parathiso*, there was bound to be a stool somewhere for me.

SKIATHOS V. SKOPELOS

*Rouvades: a secret word invented by the Skiathans
to describe the Skopelites' stupidity.*

Skiathan legend

Ask a Skiathan what he thinks of Skopelos Island, its neigh-bor to the east:

"Not friendly like Skiathos."

"No good beaches."

"Not as green as Skiathos."

Ask a Skopeliti what he thinks of Skiathos:

"Too crowded."

"Too many tourists."

"The food is not fresh."

Separated by only seven miles of water, the two islands have been fiercely competitive since the Neolithic era. Local folklore has it that the Skopelites were jealous of the Skiathans because Skiathos had a deep harbor sheltered by several small islands that allowed large kayikis to load and unload their goods pro-tected from the strong south wind, the Skopelites' bane. It was before recorded history, but legend has it that one day, the Skopelites set out in a hundred boats with grappling irons and chains, which they planned to attach to Tsougria, the larg-est of Skiathos' small islands, in an attempt to drag it off to their harbor. While they were attaching the grappling irons, the Skiathans held an emergency town meeting where, after talking about it at length, they decided they would swim out in the dead of night to surprise the Skopelites and heroically save their island. But then, according to the Skopelites, one Skiathan suddenly realized:

"Oh! Oh! Because we have holes in our asses we might sink!"

Another Skiathan then jumped up, "Why, we'll just stuff those holes with cotton!"

And according to the Skopelites, they did, and after a long, ferocious fight on Tsougria, the Skiathans dislodged the grappling irons and forced the Skopelites to take their chains and retreat. From that time, the Skiathans were called babakokouli, cotton-asses, by their neighbors, while the Skiathans regarded the Skopelites as beneath stupid for ever thinking they could steal an island. But say what you will, the Skopelites never tried to steal any of those little islands again.

You might remember the island of Skopelos had been my first choice on our way to no place in particular, but Anthea strongly preferred Skiathos, and to me the differences didn't seem all that great, and so Skiathos it was. But over a year had passed and I still remembered the pictures of Skopelos on the Internet, where the architecture seemed more tasteful and the village more charming, and because it wasn't smothered by tourists in the summer it retained more of its quaint old-world character. After only seeing it from miles across the water, where the grass on their mountains always seemed greener, we decided to go to Skopelos for the first time on February 25th, the day they celebrate their island's patron saint and protector, Agios Riginos, who you also might remember became the reason the Skopelites believed the jealous Skiathans made up their story about the Kounistra icon so they could have a patron saint and a holiday of their own.

Riginos was the first bishop of Skopelos and supposedly a man of great learning and courage who lived in the first half of the 4th century. According to legend, there was a great dragon on Skopelos, which had its lair far from the village in a cave near the bay of Panormos. Horrific in appearance it would scramble through the countryside, smashing *kalivis* with its huge tail, eating sheep and goats and, whenever possible, humans which it would crunch between its jaws. In fact, it had so terrorized the island that it was considered the reason for a severe depopulation, because so many people had either been eaten or fled. The dragon was so notorious that neighboring islands would even send criminals condemned to death to Panormos, for the dragon to eat, thus relieving themselves of the responsibility of having to execute them. When Riginos arrived on the island to take up his bishopric, he had already decided the dragon must be destroyed and, even though many men, even bands of hired soldiers, had failed to slay the monster, he knew that he had been called to do the deed. Landing on the beach at Panormos, Riginos fell to his knees in agony at his fate and called loudly to God:

"Eleos!" Mercy.

As his shipmates departed from the shore, Riginos went off in search of the dragon. After but a few steps, behind a huge boulder, the Bishop supposedly met the dragon. What happened then remains a mystery. There were no witnesses immediately about and Riginos was forever silent on the subject. Some people thought the bishop, famous for his sermons, preached hellfire and damnation to the dragon, whereupon the monster fled, followed by Riginos, who continued his fiery oration until finally reaching a high cliff on the coast, where the dragon, rather than having to endure the lecture any longer, leapt to his death. At that same moment, according to the legend, there was an earthquake, which opened the cliff and swallowed the dragon deep inside a huge fissure, which can be seen from the sea today and is called Drakontoskisma, Dragon Schism. The spot where Riginos cried out to God is named Eleos, after his cry. Refusing to convert to paganism when Julian the Apostate was Emperor (361-363), Riginos was taken to the Old Bridge just outside the village of Skopelos and was beheaded.

In 1068, William, the powerful king of Sicily, a great collector of holy relics, had his soldiers dig up Riginos' body. Witnessed by the entire population of the helpless and outraged islanders, his body was taken to Cyprus. In 1740, a monk from Skopelos was sent to bring it back, but he was only allowed to recover Riginos' right hand, which is still kept in a box in the main church in the village. On February 25th, the day of his beheading, the Skopelites have honored him for centuries with a procession through the town to his church, several miles away, during which the hand is on display. Like the celebration at Kounistra on Skiathos, during that night the faithful camp around the church, where service and celebration take place until the morning, when the hand is returned in a procession to its secure home in the village. And this year, we were going to be there. Waiting for the hydrofoil under a scatter of midmorning clouds at the port, I was a little glum. The book store had suddenly decided to become a gift shop and I had been startled to discover five days ago there were no papers for sale, an incalculable loss. I read the New York Times and Washington Post every morning on the Internet, but to sit on the terrace with the Herald Tribune in hand was an exquisite pleasure. "Don't worry, in a day or so someone will be selling papers", the former clerk smiled and shrugged when I saw her in line to enter the hydrofoil.

Not reassured, I took my usual seat outside on the stern, where everyone went to smoke and the only place where dogs were allowed. A small curly black-haired Guido plopped at my feet and looked up at me, which suddenly made me feel worse. Vasilis, the owner of the little house by the airport, had the ugliest most vicious looking bulldog I had ever seen, a slobbering ungainly, lunging animal with a constant stream of drool, that was kept chained in a corner of the yard inside his own fence. It had recently died and Vasilis solemnly told me he could never have another. The loss had been too painful.

In fifteen minutes, the hydrofoil was across the channel and dockside at the port of Glossa, the smaller of the two villages on Skopelos, where three fishermen were lazily washing down their boat with seawater. I immediately felt a startling difference in energy, slower, quieter, gentler, which made Skiathos seem bustling. After several passengers departed, the hydrofoil continued another half hour until we approached the large, clumsy breakwater into Skopelos harbor, precisely where, if the ancient Skopelites had been successful, the little island of Tsougria would now be resting. The village itself cascaded charmingly down a hillside to the port, where most of the shops and tavernas on the quay were closed, and the two or three that were open seemed strangely quiet for such a holiday. The service at the Church of Agios Riginos was scheduled to end shortly, so we quickly found a taxi and raced along a country road for about four miles to a small parking area. Taking Anthea's arm, we hurried along a cobblestone path up a hill, passing a huge orchard of almond trees in full pink and white bloom to the sunny courtyard, where four altar boys in gold robes, holding lamps on poles and a fifth with a cross, were lining up in anticipation of the procession back to town. There is only one denomination on a small island in Greece and everyone belongs, although not everyone showed up to celebrate the patron saint and protector on this day.

The small stone church was barely overflowing as we joined a group who went in by the front steps, kissed a few icons in addition to the reliquary which held the hand, lit a candle or two, then squeezed out the side door and down the steps into the courtyard in, altogether, four minutes. As Anthea paused a moment before starting down the steep steps, a young woman in her thirties took her arm startling her. For the first time in her life, in the eyes of this Good Samaritan, she was now an

old woman, one who, like a child, might need help down the
stone steps. At the bottom, Anthea, looking slightly dazed by
the realization, thanked the woman and took my arm. Then
the church bells rang and the doors opened and the people
poured out as the procession had now begun, so we hurried
back down the hill and into a cab to take us back to the port
where we planned to have a wonderful leisurely lunch while we
waited for the procession to pass by.

At the port, there were still only a few people, a rather disappointing turnout.

Because on Skiathos the Kounistra celebration was an occasion attended by nearly the whole village, I wondered if having
two villages on the island dissipated the sense of community. I
also wondered if the story of the dragon wasn't true, and how
could it be, then all the murderers sent there for their death
must have lived and some of these people had to be their de-
scendents.

A small group of young people strolled to and fro, dressed
as if from last night's prom. One or two looked ridiculous in
cheap faux furs, a rural farmer's idea of grand style, and I felt
embarrassed for them. We took a ringside seat at a taverna after
reading its large menu posted in front, but they weren't serving
the omelets as advertised and whatever else we ordered seemed
to be off the menu until summer, so we were forced to settle
for a frozen cheese pie out of the microwave and a glass of
thin white wine as we sat in the warm sun and waited for the
procession. And waited. And had a second wine. And waited.
Then we paid our check and strolled through the rather charm-
less randomly designed village where, even after being directed
twice, we couldn't find the newspaper stand among the half
dozen stores that were open, so we retired to a ringside seat at
another café on the procession route, where we ordered dessert and espresso and waited through a second espresso. Finally,

there seemed to be a buzz and the procession came into view with the three priests chanting, one carrying the hand in its box, the five altar boys, a policeman, a fireman, a coast guard captain and perhaps thirty villagers who shuffled behind and continued on to the church on a hill overlooking the port.

There was no Skopelos Philharmonic Band, no Jimmie at the lead, no thousand of the faithful, no shotgun blasts, fireworks, no magical icon of the Panayia with tears in her eyes, just a hand in a box and a gaggle of the deeply faithful. Anthea and I looked at each other. Then she smiled, Cheshire-like. She was right about Skiathos. She knew I knew I was wrong about Skopelos. It was a dud. Depressing. The lack of energy was suffocating. There were still a dozen people in the café while we waited for the hydrofoil back to Skiathos, but they were waiting as well, and as we pulled out towards the long ungainly breakwater, I noticed there wasn't a single soul left in our café and only a few on the whole quay in the early afternoon of this most important holiday. Anthea remarked she thought the Skiathans better looking, healthier looking, and with more style. They were warmer. Smarter. Happier. But then again, she had become a Skiathan. As for me, I wouldn't be sucked in by those green mountains again. We were on our way home. The luck of the draw. I was so grateful. We might still be wandering the earth shopping for a life: Italy, France, the Orient, travelling lighter with fewer boxes.

As the hydrofoil skimmed the open sea and I watched the island recede, Cavafy's *Ithaca* came into my mind and I wondered if we had chosen Skopelos, perhaps the journey in search of a life would have been the reward. Who can say, even now, which would have been better? What sights and sounds, tastes and pleasures, had we missed? Or maybe it doesn't make a difference anyway. We all carry a cross on whichever road and do our best to live with the hand we've been dealt. Maybe the real reward is simply the journey from cradle to grave, which may or not be the final destination which, as Cavafy says, may or may not give you the riches you anticipate.

At the port in Skiathos, we ran into Geoff, who told us the liquor store would be selling the newspapers the following day.

TWO GOAT HERDERS FROM HOLLYWOOD

They were, after all, only goats,
as untrustworthy and unruly as small children.

Alexandros Papadiamantis

Sometime during that first autumn when our house was being built, I watched a man on a neighboring hillside make
an acre of brambles and weeds look like a manicured lawn, as
well as prune fifty olive, a half dozen fig and pear trees, trim
and cut the branches into firewood and burn the rest, and all
in three days, working *siga siga* but carefully and steadily eight
hours a day, pausing every twenty-five minutes for a five-min-
ute cigarette break, standing tall staring out at the sea with
the same sweet satisfaction as young Yiannis the fisherman. I
met him on the road one day and discovered his English was
surprisingly good. He said, to my enduring shame, that he had
picked it up by "listening on the street". Even though he had
a great deal of work scheduled, he agreed to take a few days to
make our land look like our neighbor's, which he did.

Living in the Garden of Eden was a little bit like Midas and
gold. Everything you touched grew, and remarkably quickly,
which was both good and bad news. The good news was you
felt as though you had suddenly developed a green thumb no
matter how many cultivated plants you'd destroyed in your life.
The bad was the inhospitable weeds and brambles that grew
and multiplied at a feverish pace, growing waist high in a few
months, and you needed someone like Yiannis a minimum of

once a year, preferably between November 1st and May 1st, when burning was allowed on the island.

This year, I called Yiannis in November. He promised to schedule me. I called in December. I was on the schedule for January, he assured me. I called in February a number of times. He didn't answer and there was no way to leave a message. In March I tried again. Nothing. The land was looking increasingly neglected, so I appealed to Spiros.

"No problem. I give you goats and seeps. They clean the land fantastic."

In Greek "h" has the sound of a long "e" and since Spiros learned the word "sheep" through reading, he thought "sheep" had three e's, which so continually amused us we never corrected him. In the morning, two of his men were fencing the two acres below our house as well as any young trees and all of the figs.

"The goats, we must be careful. They eat everything, like devils" Spiros explained at the end of the day while checking the fencing.

One week later, Spiros' truck pulled up with seven goats in the bed, and two of his men dropped them one at a time over the fence. It was thrilling. Farm animals on the property! One large brown doe with an enormous udder immediately caught our attention. She had the use of only three legs, her right rear leg bent in such a way that when she was standing tall, the leg dangled at a forty-five degree angle to the ground. The sight touched us, and we earmarked her for special love and attention. The doe was much larger than the rest, who were still kids, and the kids looked to her for guidance and leadership as they quickly began nibbling the tastier bits of wild greens. We watched enchanted as they would soon tire of this green and dash over there for another, so graceful, so energetic, such manner and bearing. Maria almost burst into tears when she first saw them. They reminded her of her girlhood home in Albania and she feverishly unhitched the fence door, chased one small kid until she caught it, then picked it up and hugged it and nuzzled her face in its fur. I took pictures and sent them off on the Internet to Robert and friends I thought would be equally charmed. They were a new form of television. We would sit on the wall and drink morning coffee and watch them pick over the land. Anthea would step outside every fifteen minutes to watch the idyllic scene. Whether grazing or at rest or being milked by one of Spiros' men, our life had been immeasurably enhanced by their presence and we quickly realized again how much we enjoyed having animals around the house, Pappou notwithstanding.

After the dog, the earliest domesticated animal was the goat. Besides being a draft animal and a source of meat and milk, its skin was used for carrying water and wine and as parchment for writing and its hair was woven. It also served as a sacrificial animal to the gods, hence the scapegoat, a symbol used to bear the sins of a whole community as far back as ancient Babylon and as far forward as modern Japan. In myths and beliefs, the male goat was lust personified, the goat with a human head depicted depravity, and in Judaism the goat was an object of worship of false gods, which in Christianity became transformed into a sign of the Devil, lust, and the damned. The poor goat, relentlessly eating the brambles and weeds and giving milk and meat, the kids playing with each other, butting heads, digging in the dirt, so gentle, so dignified, had obviously gotten a bum rap.

Yiannis finally arrived in his old red truck a few days after the goats.

"A thousand pardons" he pleaded.

He'd been swamped and couldn't seem to catch up. I understood. When you were that good you were in demand, and when you lived on a small island you had to serve relatives and childhood friends first. There was still work around the perimeter of the house, which he did in a couple of days, throwing the clippings over the fence for the goats, then he apologized again and left with a pledge to return early in the fall. The day after he left, it was chilly and windy and I was feeding the roses just off the terrace when I heard a sudden loud and constant Baa!!! Baa!!! Rushing to the edge of the terrace, I looked down to see a medium sized male, his horns caught in the web of the fence, angrily baaing and whipping his head, shaking the fence so hard I thought he would rip it out of its mooring.

Having never been close to a hysterical animal with horns large enough to call to Euboea, I nonetheless raced down the two flights of steps, then tiptoed to the fence calling gently:

"Nice boy, nice boy" which only seemed to further enrage him.

Watching almost a minute while the buck pulled the fence apart, frozen with doubt, still calling "nice boy, nice boy", I finally screwed up my courage and petted him, which meant nothing to him. Becoming encouraged by that small bit of bravery, I took one of his horns with my hand. Quickly realizing he was much too strong to handle with one hand, I became suddenly empowered and grabbed the horns with both hands and with all my might seized his thrashing head and began wrestling his horns out of the mesh, first freeing one then quickly enmeshing it again as I tried to free the other, adrenalin running wild, until both horns were free. The buck wrenched out and away and left me standing tall and strong, a new hyphen after my name, goat herder. The next day, Spiros' truck pulled up with a half dozen sheep and the two men herded them easily through the gate, where they quickly settled and immediately began grazing. If only I could paint. Late that afternoon, Anthea called down to me from her studio: "I hear the animals and they seem very near."

I stepped outside and indeed they did sound very near. In

fact, standing in our rose garden, being led by the big doe, the small herd of goats was merrily munching the new leaves.

"YAAAAA!!!" was my first reaction, which panicked them and sent them sprinting down the driveway. I dashed back into the house and picked up the fly swatter. "Call Spiros!" I yelled as I chased after them swatting the air, stepping on little black pebbles of goat shit in my good moccasins. One thing I quickly learned about being a goat herder is that you can't do it alone. When you approach them, the goats will run. No matter how softly I drew near, when I came within a few feet they would bound away.

"Spiros is sending somebody!" Anthea called down from her studio window as I ran by chasing the goats up the mountain road.

I had to stop and catch my breath. I was a human; surely I could outsmart a bunch of goats. Fifteen minutes more of chasing them up and down the mountain road before Spiros' truck pulled up with two of his men who jumped out and gingerly approached them, softly calling:

"Ella ella", come come.

Because it was the call for them to feed or to be milked, the goats stood confused for a moment, but didn't run and were gently persuaded back to the gate, which they bounded through like errant children. It was simple I deduced, simply stand in their way and take a step towards them when you want them to turn.

The gate had been secure. The men tracked the goat shit from the rose garden down the flights of steps, looking for the escape route but they lost the trail. They walked the fence for a break, but couldn't find one. After a consultation, they determined it must have been the space under the fence near the stairs where the buck caught his horns, which seemed high and wide enough to allow them to crawl through. Although it seemed hardly possible for the fat lame doe, they nevertheless blocked the space with stones, milked the goats and left.

"*Diavoli!*" Maria laughed the next day.

"Devils" Anthea translated.

By now, Maria was taking home a gallon of the goats' milk a week and making cheese and cheese pies, some for us, and we all continued in pastoral heaven without incident for another few days, when once again Anthea called down from her studio:

"The goats sound awfully close."

I grabbed a broom and ran onto the terrace to see the little devils among the young fruit trees, nibbling the tender green leaves. As soon as I appeared, they dashed away. "Call Spiros" I yelled as I slowly and inoffensively followed the goats in my slippers through a field of little black balls of dung, gently calling "Ella, ella, ella."

The goats of course ignored me, but finally stopped on the road to graze until I caught up with them, then they ran down the hillside up the driveway to the fruit trees when I called to Anthea to chase them back down the driveway where I would maneuver them towards the gate. Shy at first at having yet another career, Anthea nonetheless eventually made noises sending the goats towards me. As they approached, I also made noises and stomped on the ground redirecting them towards the fence. Then Anthea raced down the steps to cut them off, while I unhitched the gate, and as I stood holding the door, the goats leapt past me into the enclosure and immediately lay under an olive tree in the shade, thirsty and tired, but happy. The sheep fifty feet away didn't seem to notice.

Another search of the fence found no breach, except maybe one spot, which I thought might just have been big enough for the determined big doe to squeeze under. "Not possible" Anthea shook her head.

I blocked it with stones and we hoped the little devils were finally secured. But it happened again in a few days. And again. By now, Anthea with a fly swatter and I with the broom, had become quite adept at wrangling the goats back through the gate. It was fun to do and we laughed the whole time. On the other hand, we were becoming increasingly housebound, afraid the little imps were waiting for us to leave so they could eat what was left of our now pathetic garden. I appealed once again to Spiros. After checking the entire fence line and agreeing there was no possible opening big enough for the doe to crawl under, he pointed to an olive tree near the fence:

"They climbing that tree. Then jump over."

Anthea gave me a look, "Spiros, she's lame."

"She still has three legs", Spiros laughed.

It wasn't possible. The old lame doe couldn't possibly have negotiated her fat body up the tree and over the fence. She was neither agile nor athletic. In fact, she hardly ever moved, lying down, chewing on whatever was nearest to her. For the first few days we even thought she was sick. But for Spiros there was no other explanation and the boys fenced the tree. Days went by without incident. The goats stayed penned and ate constantly along with the sheep and the land was becoming clean. Large patches of reddish brown earth soon appeared. One afternoon, Anthea looked out the window of her studio and saw a dozen goats on the hillside above our house, eating the tender little leaves off our baby walnut trees. We immediately snapped into action. Anthea grabbed the swatter and ran down the stairs, I grabbed the broom and we met on either side of the herd.

"They're not ours", Anthea looked puzzled.

It was true. God knows whose they were but they weren't ours. By now, they were cozying up to our goats along the fence, sniffing each other and Baaaing.

"Now what?" I didn't know where to begin.

"Follow the shit", Anthea fired back.

I followed the little black dung balls up the road until they disappeared into the forest. Then I ran back to Anthea and, after several wrong turns, we finally herded them back into their exit point and made fierce sounds and slapped trees until they disappeared. We waited a minute, occasionally slapping and growling, hoping we frightened them back to wherever they came from. For the next three days, we stayed close to home in various stages of alert, but they never returned.

Another week went by without another goat incident and we were beginning to agree that Spiros might have been right. The goats and sheep had been eating their way down the hillside, never mingling, as they became smaller and less visible. One particularly hot day, I stepped out on the terrace to look for the animals. The sheep were lifelessly eating in one corner while the goats had moved mostly out of view. As I turned to leave, I noticed something big and brown that seemed to be in one of the olive trees further down the hillside. Grabbing my binoculars, I leaned over the railing. Focused. Six feet off the ground in the crotch of a big old olive tree, the old lame doe was lying on her back, lazily nibbling the tender leaves.

"*Diavoli*", I muttered, having learned a new word.

I now knew the difference between sheep and goats and, as I encountered people during my day, I would categorize them as one or the other. Now that I understood the basis of goat myths and beliefs, I decided if I had a choice of one or the other, there would be no choice. The goats were clearly more beautiful and clearly more fun: prancing, dashing, jumping, butting, lawless and independent, untrustworthy and unruly as small children. Spiros said that after the animals had eaten all the briars and weeds and fertilized the land, the earth would become black and fertile and next spring it would be filled with the best edible wild greens and flowers. I couldn't wait.

HOLIDAY OF HOLIDAYS

I said to the almond tree, "Sister, talk to me about God."
And the almond tree blossomed.

Nikos Kazantzakis

A s the days grew longer and warmer, the first fig and grape vine leaves appeared, red poppies again began dotting the fields, the Judas trees bloomed bright pink and the fruit trees flowered, the first artichokes and broad beans and mange-tout peas and wild asparagus became ready for eating. I began to hear the sound of frogs and the night call of the Scops Owl for the first time since November. The earth was bursting with energy and the air was suddenly filled with butterflies, Swallowtails, Clouded Yellows, Painted Ladies, Red Admirals, Large and Small Coppers, Camberwell Beauties, Large Blue, Cabbage White, and as productive as the earth had suddenly become it was an equally productive time for Skiathans.

Everyone in almost every household was suddenly sanding or painting, scrubbing or scouring, planting, pruning, there was suddenly even a whole army of workers picking litter off the sides of the road, olive trees were pruned, land was cleaned, garden soil turned and plied with goat manure brought by the truckload, vegetables planted. The air was electric and the island was lush with wildflowers, and because the tourist season hadn't yet started and the weather was perfect and the work was mostly out of doors, it was without exception everyone's favorite time of year. Because most on the island earned part of their living from tourism, the villagers made the outside of their houses as charming and beautiful and as "Greek Village" as possible, which only lent to the already intrinsic charm. The businesses that depended on tourism, which in every category every year became increasingly competitive, all worked tirelessly to prepare for Palm Sunday, the Sunday before Easter, when the island would begin filling with strangers from all over the world, who would come to enjoy a little piece of Greece. Then there was Anthea, attempting to paint the view to Euboea upstairs in her studio, grumpy and complaining about how untalented she was, then cheerfully making me wonderful lunches and dinners, always arranging my plate carefully and tastefully, as if I were dining at some wonderful restaurant. And I was. And me, reading Heroditus for the first time out on the terrace, feet on the wall, looking off past the sea to the endless mountains she was now trying to paint, learning that Helen never made it to Troy with Paris but was kept under house arrest in Egypt by its king, Proteus, for defiling her home, but Homer thought it a better story to continue her on to Troy. Laying the history on my lap and looking at my toes, I wished the days would last forever, a picture postcard time. The land was clean and the goats and sheep were under control. Our two guest rooms had been reserved for friends and family at intervals for the next four months, and we were looking forward to the visits. More and more I was realizing the privileged life we were leading, in every aspect: love, health, wealth and position. And yet underlying it all was the knowledge that it wouldn't last forever. Like Mihalis, who never read Proust, would occasionally say:

"You don't know, your life could end in a half hour."

So I basked in it, hoping against hope I was not giving myself the evil eye, just allowing myself to enjoy what I had while I had it.

The Greeks enjoyed a long history of celebrating spring beginning with the *Anthesteria Dionysia*, the ancient Dionysian Festival of the Flowers, which opened with a drinking contest and was one of the two occasions during the year when Greek women were allowed to leave the house and participate in public life, dance wildly, drink wine, and even eat the raw meat of animals they killed. On Skiathos, from as early as the 6th century B.C., when its wine and oil were famous and exported throughout the Mediterranean, the god of wine and oil, Dionysus, was the island's heavenly patron and the festival in his honor had an even greater significance. After twenty-six hundred years, it appeared that Anthesteria Dionysia had survived in the form of Carnival Week, which began on Carnival Sunday, when Greeks of all ages dressed in costumes and told off-color jokes, often involving the clergy, who were sometimes referred to as bearded old goats. Sexually suggestive songs were even playing on public radio all week, which Anthea gleefully translated:

I touched her shoulder, she said
Lower.
I touched her waist, she said
Lower.
I touched her knee, she said
Higher.

Everyone seemed to be blowing off steam, especially towards the Church, as a way to gird up for the Great Fast ahead, no meat or dairy for seven weeks, which would become even more restrictive the final week before Easter Sunday, the most important holiday of the Greek calendar. Of course not everyone observed the fast, but enough did so that there was almost no fresh meat in the markets during those weeks. The end of

Carnival Week was *Tirofago Kyriaki* or Cheese Eating Sunday, which marked the day before the fast, when Greeks ate up all the milk and cheese in their house, and which provided yet another occasion for the Skiathos Philharmonic Band, the children, and the grown up children to parade to the end of the port and back.

This year the air was balmy, the sky was clear and the sun was warm and welcoming as it sparkled like a huge golden crystal on a bright blue sea. Plastic clowns hung on all the light poles at the port, where Anthea and I arrived an hour early to meet Geof and Lida and other friends, including John and Erini, architects who lived in one of the row houses across from Windsor Castle that had been built for Queen Victoria's ladies in waiting, and who owned a charming summer house on the island. He, a tall, full of vinegar Irish Republican, she, a slender but tough Greek lefty. In sharp contrast to that lusterless holiday in Skopelos, most of the tavernas and cafés were open and dozens of long tables were already filled to capacity with Skiathan families drinking ouzo or coffee and greeting each other:

"*Chronia pola.*"

It was John who noticed a stack of chairs and tables leaning against the wall of a small taverna that hadn't yet opened, so he grabbed a table in each hand and set them in a rather good viewing spot midway on the parade route as two Skiathos Police, a man and a woman, chatting not thirty feet away, glanced indifferently. After commandeering ten chairs, we notified the neighboring taverna we were ready to order and were being served an excellent omelet when we heard the sound of the band and the applause as Jimmie came into view, marching proudly in his brown suit and red tie. He was followed by the leader of the Skiathos Philharmonic followed by the Band, ever concentrating on their playing and marching precision, followed by groups of grinning children marching by grade, each with their own costumes, beginning with preschoolers dressed as mermaids and fisherman and ending with the high school seniors as smarmy *bouzouki*-joint types with painted on mustaches, followed by children of all ages, the men and women from the Garden Club dressed as seasonal vegetables, an old man dressed as a woman with balloons for breasts, a young woman dressed as a priest reading a copy of Playboy and, interspersed with all of the above, excellent floats on wagons pulled by tractors and flat bed trucks, Barbarossa's pirate ship, a Dionysian festival with people in togas and crowns of olive wreaths, drinking wine and throwing olive leaves.

There were so many Skiathans in the parade it seemed a marvel there was anyone to watch, yet the quay was filled and there was much applause and laughter and many names were called out as people on both sides waved and took pictures. As the orchestra reached the end of the parade route, I remembered thinking it seemed that the better measurement of life than time was the fullness of moments, so that one full moment would equal two moments only half full and, using that as a criterion, I decided that if I had the ability to share only five moments with all the people I loved, I might have chosen any part of that twelve minutes as one of my five.

After the parade, our group adjourned to Vromolimnos, a beautiful sheltered white sand beach which in summer was the playground for young singles but was now deserted. Again an unopened taverna provided two tables and a dozen chairs. We set the tables in the shade of a big pine tree, built a fire in the sand to fry fresh Skiathan sausages and bread, and laid out the salads and fruits, all the while consuming much wine and talking world politics until early evening, when the sun finally disappeared, and all the while thinking yet again "Lord, I am not worthy."

Although she had no contact with the Greek community in our thirty years together and disdained any kind of religion, and even slammed the nearest table at least two or three times a year shouting "They should be outlawed!", Anthea was now being drawn back to the simplicity and wisdom of *Yiayia* Maria's ways. Since the celebration at Kounistra, beneath her great style and wit, the small Greek child had been emerging, and because she had become aware of my complete apostasy, she was becoming increasingly vulnerable and wary of my re- action to her journey, especially after I several times jokingly referred to her as "born again" and on her way to becoming "one of those old ladies in black picking salad greens by the side of the road", a foot-in-mouth habit I inherited from my mother. So being a Greek and feeling the need to observe the Great Fast, she very cleverly and subtly in the several weeks preceding referred to my ever-gathering girth, on the average of one pound a month since our arrival. Then, over dinner one night, she offered me a Trojan horse: "It might be a good idea for both of us to go on a diet for a while, six or seven weeks. Cleanse our bodies. Cut out the meat and chicken. We should probably try and cut down on the cheese, too. And, if we're up to the challenge, why we might even cut out oil in the last week." She smiled, knowing the vain fat man would think it an excellent idea without ever realizing the Orthodox context. And so we began.

Although the Orthodox diet forbade fish other than shell- fish, Anthea and I ate all kinds of fish and vegetables for the next six weeks. In fact, I ate more fish than in my entire life. But, instead of shedding, I was adding at an alarming rate: pas- ta four times a week, a mountain of bread and chocolate, and loukoums. I was losing control and looking alarmingly like Ro- din's sculpture of Balzac. I needed meat. And chicken. I never imagined myself missing chicken and yet I craved it more than meat. And more cheese. It was only a few days into our diet when this genius realized it was the Byzantine fast (they don't call it Byzantine for nothing) and I would be forever on my guard against Trojan horses. But I didn't say anything. I didn't complain. Anthea knew but said nothing. Instead, she became even more imaginative, trying to make the seven seasonal vegetables available in the market together with yet another kind of fish seem like a Bacchanalian feast. But I could tell by her glance that she knew the screws were loosening and my will to resist a pork gyro was weakening by the day and there was still one more week.

At some point, she began to realize that, although I had ceased to accept the theology, I still believed very strongly in a spiritual component in the universe, and I understood and welcomed whatever contact she wanted with the Church. So on Palm Sunday, in my church clothes, I lit a candle at the cathedral which was strewn with bay leaves, since palms were not indigenous to Greece, then stood in the doorway of Stamatis' bakery while he leaned on the counter with his chin on his hands, watching the other men in groups, smoking and subtly kicking and playing with the bay leaves covering the square with their feet. Stamatis had married a girl he met while she was on a holiday in Skiathos. After extracting a promise before they were married that she would never leave the island, they had two children. Within a few years she became bored and returned to France with the children, leaving him broken hearted but not bitter, and with plenty of extra time to learn the *bouzouki*, which he practiced tirelessly. As with all traumatic events which shape your point of view, Stamatis was today reflecting on the life of the Greek ship owner whose mega-yacht was in the port below:

"A little house, a little land, a little money, a little company, what more do you want?"

For the first time in thirty-six days, the no-fish-other-than-shellfish rule was suspended, a special day, so after church we gathered with Spiros and the family at their *kalivis* around a table under a newly sprouting grape vine, while Spiros was basting a dozen sea bass on a small barbeque. It was the first outdoor meal of the season which made it all the more splendid.

For Anthea, even as a child growing up in Brooklyn, there was no Easter Bunny, no basket of chocolate eggs and candy. Yet, Easter was the most important holiday of the year. The season began with Carnival Week, included Palm Sunday, and ended on Easter Sunday with the actual celebration beginning on Holy Thursday, the Thursday morning before Easter, and ending with the Easter feast, which ended the great fast. Because this year Anthea wanted to attend all the major Easter services, we made a date to meet Spiros and his family for Thursday's mass at the Evangelistria Monastery at 7:00 a.m.

Dedicated to the Annunciation of the Virgin, it was the island's main monastery and was founded in 1794 by an ordained monk named Niphon, from Athos, who wanted to return to the original Orthodox tradition. In 1795, twenty highly educated monks who were aristocrats and philosophers also arrived from Athos. During the dark years of the Ottoman rule, the monks taught the Greek classics and Byzantine values in hidden schools, crypha scholia, in the monasteries, which enabled the Greeks to retain their language, religion, and ethnic identity. In Skiathos, the philosopher monks had a profound influence, especially on native sons such as writers Alexandros Papadiamantis and his cousin Alexandros Moraitidis, and Skiathos became known as The Island of Scholars. The monastery was also instrumental in the pre-revolutionary planning, as well as the revolution in 1821, when the Greeks finally won their independence from the Turks. It was there that the first Greek flag with the white cross on a blue background was designed, woven, blessed, and raised. It was on this flag that Father Niphon swore in the guerrilla leaders, including the great leader of the revolution, Theodore Kolokotronis, following the great assembly held at the monastery to lay out plans to liberate the nation.

Orthodox churches are in the shape of a perfect cross with the altar in the middle, the priests' room in the back, chairs in front, and against the two adjacent walls a single line of chairs with two sets of arm rests, one while sitting and the other while standing. In Skiathos there were usually more people than chairs, more people standing than could sit, and little children weren't required to be still, but walked around and looked at things or played quietly on the floor, a formal service in a relaxed atmosphere, piety without display, attendance at any moment purely voluntary. As we entered the church and I watched Spiros, Matoula and Anthea kiss the same spot of glass which separated the painted icon from the lips of every parishioner who kissed it when entering, it occurred to me this custom must have been the world's first flu shot.

Spiros went to one of the adjacent walls where three men were chanting and singing responses to Papa Angelos, a middle-aged balding ordained monk with a short black beard, and motioned for me to follow. I had now been to a few Orthodox services but until that moment I was never any closer than the furthest away of the faithful. I had never been near the altar, but Spiros' silent insistence in addition to my recent Athos experience gave me the courage to step in front of the others to join him.

There were many similarities between the Greek Orthodox Mass and the old Roman Catholic Latin Mass of my childhood, in which I spent so much time singing hymns and responses in the choir loft at St. Monica's Church in Vermont. Two masses every morning, 6:30 and 7:30, I received ten cents per mass and sang one for free on Sunday with the larger choir; so it was with great nostalgia that I was standing next to the chorus when I noticed tears streak down Papa Angelos' cheeks. Later,

Spiros told me that Papa Angelos always cried when he sang about Christ's passion and death, but he thought the priest was just acting. I explained to Spiros that in my experience as an actor one couldn't cry real tears without outside help, unless in that moment he was feeling that kind of sorrow. Reflecting a moment he said:

"Thank you for telling me that."

After the service, we drove to the village to Loula's for a special lunch, which was traditional in Skiathos on Holy Thursday: fresh local lobster, in the season when, everyone agreed, they tasted the sweetest. While walking through the narrow cobblestone streets, we encountered clusters of small children dressed in Sunday clothes, carrying crosses made of flowers to commemorate Christ carrying the cross. Visiting the houses, they would sing a hymn for sweets and money:

Today the heavens are black, today a black day,

Today everyone is grieving and the mountains are sorrowful.

After my experience with the old lady in black last Christmas, I was now prepared on these occasions and always had several coins at the ready.

At Loula's, the children were dying eggs red, because Thursday was also the day of the Last Supper and the tradition is to dye eggs to represent Christ's blood. The eggs would be cracked on Easter Sunday and the one with the last egg uncracked was destined to have good fortune and the best of health throughout the year.

As we were eating, Spiros laughingly told us how, after having tracked down and secured the twelve finest freshest lobsters for the meal, they had been delivered to him at his store the day before at about 5 o'clock. They had been sitting outside the entrance on the floor of his jeep, wrapped in ice for an hour in several red plastic bags, waiting for Matoula to pick them up, when he spotted Panayotis, a fat old man with manic eyes, walking past the store wearing a windbreaker, holding himself as he gave a worried glance inside and hurried on his way. Spiros immediately had a bad feeling. He dropped the phone and rushed out to the jeep. The bags were there but the lobsters were gone. He looked down the street.

Panayotis had vanished. Panicked, Spiros dashed back into his store, called his neighbor, Tassos, and asked him if he had seen Panayotis go by. Tassos said he always kept an eye out for Panayotis because he always stole something from his store and, just a minute ago, he watched him run by and throw something under an unhitched trailer up the street. A moment later, Spiros and Tassos met at the unhitched trailer where, surprise, under the trailer in blue plastic bags swiped from Tassos' store, the twelve big beautiful lobsters Panayotis must have been hiding under his jacket when Spiros had seen him hurry past the door. He and Tassos exchanged the plastic bags with the lobsters with similar bags filled with rotten fruit and dog shit and put them back under the trailer with a lobster claw sticking out of each bag so that Panayotis wouldn't think to look inside until he got home. Panayotis hadn't returned by the time Spiros and Tassos closed their stores for the evening but Spiros laughed for a long moment at what he thought would be Panayotis' reaction. And now the famous lobsters, boiled with fresh wild greens, were on the table, where almost every age was represented and every type in an extended family, and for a moment, as I laughed along with the others, I found myself transported back to Vermont where as a boy I would sit at my grandfather's large table for a holiday meal, while the women cleared the table and set out the desserts, only now I was one of the old people.

After dinner, a complete fast would begin for Spiros and his family, no more food until after midnight mass early Sunday morning, but not for us. Fish. For two more days. Then real food. I was beginning to think I might make it, although I might not have a pair of pants for the service on Sunday.

Thursday midnight at the cathedral, Anthea and I were among an overflow crowd holding lighted candles in a gentle spring breeze. Peering through the side door while the church bells rang and the choir sang, I could see Papa Yiorgos, looking like Santa Claus with his long white beard and gold rimmed spectacles, carrying the church's three and a half foot cross, followed by Papa Nikolas, stopping in front of different icons where Papa Yiorgos read a different prayer, after which the faithful lined up to kiss the feet of the Christ, a booster shot. Those who wanted to give special thanks hung a wreath of flowers on the cross. These rituals were such an integral part of the Skiathans' life, beginning as little children holding their candles, fascinated by the flame, listening to the chants and hymns they had heard from their first memory of Easter and would hear throughout their life. There was so much beauty in the service: the flowers, the bells, the choir, the pageantry, the candles, the incense, the wide eyes of the children, the piousness of the old women dressed in black, the generational continuity of father and son priests. Although seven year old Apostoles' lips moved along with the choir as he held his candle, he was much less fascinated by the flame than by his uncle, Papa Nikolas, as he swung the censor, and his grandfather, Papa Yiorgos, as he carried the big cross and moved from icon to icon, and I strongly suspected yet another generation would be represented on that altar. I was enjoying the services. Not feeling compelled to do more than light a candle and then step outside with the smokers, they became pleasant social events in lofty settings.

Friday night's service was my favorite. It began at Evangelistria Monastery at around 10:00 p.m. We decided to get there a half hour early to get a good view, perhaps even a seat, but the crowd had already grown considerably. The church was bursting and the large courtyard was overflowing into the surrounding grounds and even into the road. We did manage to watch through a window as a large wooden figure of Christ was unscrewed from the wooden cross and the priests, dressed in black, wrapped the body in a golden shroud and placed it on the altar. Then, six men, the pall bearers, entered the main body of the church from the foyer, carrying the Epitaphios, a tomb for the figure, completely covered in flowers and lit with candles, where the priests placed the figure of Christ wrapped in his gold shroud inside and threw rose petals on it while the choir sang hymns. The Epitaphios was then carried by the six men out of the church, through the courtyard and up a long series of old stone steps to a path which wound through the forest, followed by the entire congregation carrying lit candles. I stood with my candle close to the new mayor's fisherman father, who looked strangely wolf-like with a Bruce Springsteen jaw, flashing eyes and oversized teeth. With a voice like a ship's horn he bellowed out the next hymn line, and the whole procession then sang the line over a very simple melody. We all continued this way along the mountain for an hour or more in pitch darkness but for the candles and the moon, the mayor's father stopping every few lines so as to blend in deep rich harmony with four other older men, including myself. The scene transported me once again to my choir days as a boy on Easter Sunday, the one mass when the boys' choir was privileged to sing with the men's choir, where my father was the choirmaster. It was a rare and glorious experience for me, and I couldn't help but get carried away and sing too loudly, whereupon my father would give me his angry glance and I would immediately bring down my volume. I was probably trying to get his attention in order to share the glorious moment. Perhaps the difference between being a child and an adult is that the child is free to exult in any given moment, while the adult is too busy trying to cover his ass. Then again I decided that I was perhaps thinking too much about my father and that I should just let him rest in peace.

Happily, however, in that particular Greek chorus it seemed there was no such thing as too loudly. Skiathans, it seemed to me, didn't have what singers called a head voice, usually softly sung and emanating above the neck. Every sound whether spoken or sung came from deep inside their chest. You never had to ask anyone to speak up, there was no need, no one mumbled. Even when saying *"Efharisto"*, thank you, to which the reply is *"Parakalo"*, you're welcome, no big deal. It roars back. Now, when speaking to a Greek, I find myself bellowing and I must admit it always feels good.

After what seemed like one of the shortest hours of my life, the procession found its way back to the monastery courtyard where the doors of the church were closed and the priest knocked three times to be let back in. Inside, one of the village elders asked through the doors who it was. After the third response, the doors opened and the Epitaphios was placed back into the center of the church. I felt like applauding, however inappropriate. The whole pageant was so stirring, the huge chorus, the spectacle of the procession, but I restrained myself as people began to stand around and chat, and we spoke briefly to Effie, and then to Tasoula and Stamatis, standing with a yawning Filaretti, before I took Anthea's arm and we walked slowly back to the jeep, tired but exhilarated.

Finally, the most celebrated day in the Greek calendar, Easter Sunday, which celebrates the resurrection of Christ and begins, of course, on Saturday night. It actually begins on Friday at Christ's Tomb in Jerusalem where, like for the Olympics, a torch is lit from an eternal flame, flown to Athens and then distributed throughout Greece. On Saturday, at eight o'clock in the evening, the flame arrived at the Skiathos airport and, after a ceremony, was taken in a procession to the cathedral. At a quarter to midnight, Anthea and I were standing on the square, leaning against the wall of Stamatis' bakery, shoulder to shoulder in the largest crowd yet, which extended down the wide stone steps to the port lined with magnificent yachts, and where there was standing room only in all the tavernas and cafés. At the stroke of midnight, all of the lights and candles in the church and the square were extinguished but for the eternal flame. With a chant that intoned each to receive light, the flame lit the priests' candles inside the church, which in turn lit the candles of those closest, who in turn did the same until everyone at the service was holding a candle, and the courtyard filled with people standing on steps all the way down to the port and to the yachts and tavernas, each in turn lighting the candle of his neighbor while the bells were ringing and the choir was singing *"Christos Anesti ek Nekron"*, Christ has Risen from the Dead, joined by the entire congregation. The sky was suddenly awash with fireworks and, with as much meaning as a thunderous Hollywood Bowl New Year's celebration, everyone kissed everyone else and wished them, *"Christos Anesti!"*, Christ has risen. It was strange, this New Year celebration at Easter, and I remembered wondering on the actual New Year's Eve why Greeks didn't make more of it. Anthea would later explain that Easter for the Greeks was more than just about religion. It was a collective social tradition, a coming together and solemnly reaffirming their commitment to their church and their nation. During the long Turkish occupation, because they were allowed to practice their religion, church feasts like Easter became the way the Greeks could express their national character, their separateness. After all, every Turk celebrated New Year's Day.

After the service, the fast could finally be broken, so the tavernas were open late and the quay was filled to overflowing. Anthea and I made our way to Loula's house through groups walking with their candles still lit en route to their small church, or roadside shrine, or simply a candle on their dresser where they would continue the flame for another year, for nearly everyone had some personal altar which contained icons of the virgin and their own particular patron or name day saint. Anthea had the sensitivity not to suggest eliminating oil in our diet that last week. I had now become a feta cheese with oil and olives addict, so it was no small relief to know I could now return to my own way of dieting, the satisfying Mediterranean diet, not too much of anything, and more exercise. And now, Loula had prepared the traditional Easter break fast, a delicate soup of finely diced lamb liver, rice and wild greens but, knowing I didn't like liver, she also breaded some pork cutlets for me. By one-thirty in the morning, I already had two helpings of cutlets, two and a half helpings of the delicious soup and drunk enough wine to worry about embarrassing myself. The egg contest was announced and my egg was the first earmarked to receive the blow. Anthea's egg smacked it but her egg cracked. I hit Mercini and cracked hers and also cracked Loula's as she tried to crack mine and, as if in slow motion, one by one I cracked all the others, or they cracked trying to crack mine, until my egg was the last uncracked egg. For the first time in my life I had won the Easter Egg Cracking Contest! All those years! I was numb! Good health and good luck for another year! I awoke the next morning in a haze out of which came the thought that Loula had won the Basilopitta on New Year's Day and had uncharacteristically slipped and fallen three times since, and I wondered if winning the egg contest made someone jealous. I spent the next few moments spitting, until I reached the kitchen where I poured water into a glass and then dropped some olive oil on top. The drops stayed on top. What a curious test! Still, I was relieved I wouldn't be needing a priest.

Easter Sunday dinner was a drive on a bumpy dirt road over the mountain to the north side of the island, which was almost totally undeveloped, where Takis was our host at his beautiful and spacious villa on a cliff overlooking the sea. I hadn't seen Takis for more than a moment since he roasted the lamb for Goldie and Kurt. He was again standing in front of a large barbeque, slow roasting a lamb and a goat on two skewers and the kokoretsi, their entrails, on two more, while chatting and laughing with a group including his sister, Chrisoula, and Spiros. Always in a hurry in the village, Takis never took his eye off the ever so slow roasting meat when Anthea and I walked onto the large terrace. Chrisoula greeted us with a tray of her cheese pie. I tasted one and I declared it was by far the best one ever and asked her if she would give Anthea the recipe:

"Oh, it's simple", her English was quite good, "First you need two liters of milk fresh from the goat in the morning, then you need one dozen eggs laid that night…"

It was another warm spring day, though clouded over, and the sea was shades of wine and blue and grey green. After we ate, we took a walk down one mountain and up another to the oldest monastery, The Panayia at Kechria, stepping through patches of chamomile, through the meadow blood-red with thousands of poppies, chervil and mallow fighting with one another for space, red mushrooms, wild grain, and flowers without names. The small monastery was deserted though several candles were burning. I was always impressed when I stepped into one of the monasteries or any of the sixty small family churches, which were nearly always deserted, but for a burning candle or two, and where icons and other items of value were left totally unguarded. Walking back along a donkey path through the pine forest, we stopped to pick a bouquet of wild-flowers, which included strands of wild asparagus, oregano, and thyme, and finally down the long cobblestone driveway to the villa with just enough energy to climb into the jeep and drive home.

Anthea was in bed by eight o'clock while I went over to John and Erini's and talked politics and drank wine, until the conversation dribbled into fragments shouted over each other among ten people, at which time we agreed to adjourn until the next time.

I was worn out from celebrating and said so when John told the story of the Venetian governor of Skyros, a neighboring is-land, who in the 16th century had to caution the Doge not to expect too much in the way of revenue from the people of these islands, because they worked only two days a week due to the fact that every other day they were celebrating some name day or festival. Then, John told me that in the morning there would be a celebration of the Feast Day of Saint George, who in icons always appears on a horse, and at approximately eleven o'clock there would be a horse race around the lake by the airport on a dirt road and the whole island would be there. Originally a race comprised of old plough horses and donkeys in honor of the saint's feast day, the prize money gradually improved under the old mayor and was now significant enough to induce serious competition among the Sporades.

The next morning, the villagers were all assembled around the small lake making friendly bets as Anthea and I squeezed in among Geof and Lida, John and Erini on top of a huge boulder of granite in front of Agios Georgios, St. George, a small fam-ily church, where the horses had been blessed in a ceremony a few minutes before. A quick report from a pistol and four horses raced into view at full throttle on a rocky dirt road no more than twenty feet wide with a crowd on both sides cheer-ing them on. It was the first of a series of heart-pounding races, the two lead horses nose to nose, and I felt anxious for the people in harms way if a rider were to lose control or a horse to stumble. But the races ended without incident and the grand winner was someone evidently close to my neighbor, Yiorgos, because afterwards he was walking the horse and rider up and down before the crowd taking bows. An hour later, feeling as though we'd run a race of our own for the last five days, we shared some white wine and a whole fish by the port, which after two days of meat was consistent with my Mediterranean diet, so I didn't resent it.

Then, like two old people, we climbed into the jeep and slowly took the mountain road home where we finally had a long, well-deserved Easter nap. Among other things, retirement can be very tiring.

ONCE YOU LIVE ON A SMALL GREEK ISLAND

A man's homeland is wherever he prospers.

Aristophanes

More than two years had passed since we had arrived on Skiathos with two suitcases and equal amounts of courage and naiveté, the two main ingredients necessary for falling in love. It had been months since we had seen Robert and now years since we laid eyes on most of the rest of our family and friends, so I called one of the Yiorgos Mitzelos, the one who, besides having a gourmet frozen food business and apartments for rent, was also a travel agent. Another strong, square, smiling Skiathan, he managed to get us two round trip tickets to Los Angeles from Athens on an American carrier which was one third less than the cheapest price for the same tickets bought in the United States.

At the same time, Anthea received an e-mail inviting her to receive a lifetime achievement award from the Costume Designers Guild for a body of work which included such films as *Chinatown* and *Rosemary's Baby*, a career she had only pursued for ten years, but which they felt deserved to be celebrated.

Since we would be in the area during the time, Anthea accepted and immediately went searching through her closet to try and find something appropriate for a fêted costume designer at a formal dress event. Having found nothing, she took one of her old dresses, which she promptly redesigned and found a seam-stress on Skiathos to alter.

Several days before we left, I volunteered to different people that I would be travelling to the United States for a month and was there something I could bring back for them?

"Blue Topsiders from Timberland" grinned Yiorgos Mitzelos, the travel agent.

"A wife", Nikos the druggist said without looking up.

"No, nothing", Angeliki the postmistress said, "Thank you very... pink lipstick."

"Pink lipstick?"

"I can't buy in Greece, this color." She showed me her nails. I winked at her; she would owe me.

"Pepto Bismol" blurted Yalis, a taverna owner who lived near us, even before I finished the question. "My stomach is bad. The only thing that works."

We packed an extra duffel for the return.

It was a long flight and because I become too anxious to sleep on an airplane, I brought Dickens' Dombey and Son, 624 pages. Dickens was simple enough for me to follow when I was restless yet could still hold my interest and, conveniently, his narrative was divided into chapters that left me hanging, making me look forward to the next, but which would allow me to take a break and walk around for a bit before diving in again. Anthea, of course, would be asleep while the plane was still on the runway. Travelling had suddenly become very frustrating. It reminded me of trying to get my visa renewed with the exception that with my visa I didn't have to take off my shoes and send them through an imaging machine. Chaos. But we were happy to be going back to well-known faces and familiar customs and Dickens was at the top of his game, because even though the ride became bumpy and I'd read it twice before, when little Dombey died I wept openly and still couldn't stop reading.

In Los Angeles, Anthea waited outside the terminal with our luggage while I took a bus to pick up a rental car we had reserved. The airport seemed so intense, the crowds, the traffic, horns, planes taking off and landing, that I found myself fretful even as I stood in the line at the rental agency. A half hour later, sitting inside the rented car, whose name I didn't recognize, I turned the radio to a familiar station which calmed me slightly as I pulled out of the parking lot and searched for the terminal. Minutes later, an airport policeman was lecturing me about leaving my car unattended as I wheeled the bags to the car and threw them into the trunk, pretending not to speak English by cheerfully nodding and gesturing and muttering the eleven words I knew in Greek, which seemed to exasperate him even further. Anthea lit a cigarette with shaking hands as we inched our way out of the airport and onto a boulevard. In a moment, we entered what two years ago was simply another freeway but now was the frighteningly chaotic San Diego Freeway, ten lanes of sixty to eighty mile an hour traffic weaving in and around each other. For over two years I had not exceeded thirty-five miles an hour on the small two-lane, mostly dirt roads in Skiathos, and I suddenly felt overwhelmed as I cautiously entered the freeway at thirty-five miles an hour in a car I had never driven before. After being nudged by several swerving cars and a double tractor-trailer air horn, I gripped the wheel and accelerated to fifty-five, the posted speed limit, one I always exceeded when I lived here like every other car whizzing past.

The freeway would be a metaphor for the rest of our trip, always in traffic, hurrying from one part of town to another or stuck in a jam, a whirlwind of breakfasts, lunches, dinners, and doctors appointments, parties, shopping trips for specific items we would ship back which we couldn't find on Skiathos, like sweet gherkins midget pickles and Paul Mitchell shampoo, with only snatches of time grabbed with Robert because he was having his own series of breakfasts, lunches and dinners.

The Costume Designers' Awards Dinner, which took place at the ballroom of the Beverly Hilton Hotel, was elegant and irreverent as usual, a preferred event among the Hollywood crowd because it's one of the few events not televised. Mike Nichols left previews of a Broadway musical he was directing to give Anthea the award. Always speaking with carefully chosen nuanced words, excellent diction and brilliant comic timing, he talked about his collaboration with her on several movies, including the one on which Anthea and I met, which was scheduled to be the studio's big Christmas release the following year. The filming was not going well. He had fired the lead actor and was casting about for a new one, when he asked Anthea what she thought of the movie, and she shrugged.

Nichols was smiling at the memory: "'You're right', I said, 'It is a shrug. But what about the millions of dollars we've already spent?' Anthea shrugged again and said 'But think of all the millions you'll save'."

Nichols paused waiting for the laugh he knew would come, then continued: "And so I called the studio and told them Anthea thinks the movie is a shrug and we should cancel the picture." Pausing for applause, he smiled, then continued, "I've always found the hardest thing to get in Hollywood is the truth," he grinned and nodded to a huge round of laughter and applause, "Which is why I always wanted Anthea beside me through the whole process."

Anthea, looking elegant and beautiful in her new old dress, gave a wonderful speech about not being afraid to be difficult because the good directors would appreciate how much you cared, and who wanted to work with the others anyway? And Robert and other family, Kurt and Goldie and many friends were there, all looking fabulous, some even suspiciously younger than I remembered. At the conclusion of Anthea's speech, everyone stood and applauded and I wondered for a moment if so much adoration was tempting her back into our old life.

Like most of our friends, Anthea and I both went to Hollywood never intending to stay. We were there for work only and when we stopped working, why we'd just go home or somewhere else, to some paradise. We never really thought it through beyond the work. Instead, in order to anchor our lives, we quickly threw down roots which, as roots do, tended to grow deeper, and supplied different needs, and as the root system grew wider it took more and more strength to sever some of them, pull others out, and transplant the rest, and, as time passed, it became harder still until finally for some it long ceased even to be a choice.

Waiting outside the hotel for our car to be delivered, we talked about how much fun the event had been, and even more so now that we were better able to see our old life in light of the larger world and the life we had just left in Skiathos. Anthea, who had always shied from the spotlight, told me she was happy it was over. I was as well. And relieved. She was as anxious to go home as I was.

Aristotle equated happiness with wisdom, which he deemed the greatest form of knowledge. Einstein thought intuition was a greater form of knowledge than intellect. If both geniuses were correct, then it would follow that wisdom must lie in intuition rather than intellect, and the pursuit to strengthen intuition must be the road to happiness. A very Platonic idea. It's all so confusing. And yet, my best life decisions were made intuitively, in less than a second, and each required stepping into the unknown, which then forced me to know myself more fully. The more I discovered about myself, the happier I became, each step expanding and refreshing my whole life as if it were dipped in a clear cool sea.

Life became even sweeter when we returned to Skiathos, friends all the more precious. Least available to us now was time. That was the most difficult. Knowing that once having found paradise it wouldn't last forever.

ACKNOWLEDGEMENTS

In addition to all of the Skiathans mentioned in this book who have enriched my life immeasurably, I wish to express my gratitude to Betsy Barnard for her invaluable research regarding the island, and Annabel Davis Goff, and Nelly Bly for their professional advice. I also wish to express my appreciation to my editors, Katerina Kaisi and Miriam Pirolo for their excellent work, and my publishers, Haris Ioannides and Aris Laskaratos for giving this writer an opportunity to be read. Finally, I wish to thank Irina Averoff, my aunt Rose, my brother, Billy, and my son, Robert, for their love and support in this effort.

ABOUT THE AUTHOR

Born in Vermont and raised in Vermont and Connecticut, Richard Romanus (1943) attended Xavier University and received a BS in Philosophy. He then attended the University of Connecticut Law School for a year, after which he left school to pursue a career as an actor. He studied at the famous Actor's Studio with Lee Strassberg and his first major role came as the character "Michael" in Martin Scorcese's classic film *Mean Streets*. In the years that followed Richard Romanus performed in numerous stage productions, films and television shows. In addition to his acting, Richard Romanus is credited as the composer on several films. Together with his wife, Anthea Sylbert, he also wrote and produced *Giving Up the Ghost* in 1998 and *If You Believe* in 1999, for which they were nominated for a Writers Guild of America award for Best Original Screenplay. Since the end of 2001 Richard and Anthea have been living in Skiathos, Greece.

ALSO BY RICHARD ROMANUS

Chrysalis